Lecture Notes in Computer Science 13734

More information about this series at https://link.springer.com/bookseries/558

Yujiu Yang · Xiaohui Wang ·
Liang-Jie Zhang (Eds.)

Cognitive Computing – ICCC 2022

6th International Conference
Held as Part of the Services Conference Federation, SCF 2022
Honolulu, HI, USA, December 10–14, 2022
Proceedings

Editors
Yujiu Yang
Tsinghua University, Shenzhen
Shenzhen, China

Xiaohui Wang
University of Science and Technology Beijing
Beijing, China

Liang-Jie Zhang ⓘ
Kingdee International Software
Group Co., Ltd.
Shenzhen, China

ISSN 0302-9743   ISSN 1611-3349 (electronic)
Lecture Notes in Computer Science
ISBN 978-3-031-23584-9   ISBN 978-3-031-23585-6 (eBook)
https://doi.org/10.1007/978-3-031-23585-6

This Springer imprint is published by the registered company Springer Nature Switzerland AG
The registered company address is: Gewerbestrasse 11, 6330 Cham, Switzerland

Preface

The 2022 International Conference on Cognitive Computing (ICCC) covered all aspects of Sensing Intelligence (SI) as a Service (SIaaS). Cognitive Computing is a sensing-driven computing (SDC) scheme that explores and integrates intelligence from all types of senses in various scenarios and solution contexts.

ICCC 2022 was one of the events of the Services Conference Federation event (SCF 2022), which had the following 10 collocated service-oriented sister conferences: the International Conference on Web Services (ICWS 2022), the International Conference on Cloud Computing (CLOUD 2022), the International Conference on Services Computing (SCC 2022), the International Conference on Big Data (BigData 2022), the International Conference on AI & Mobile Services (AIMS 2022), the International Conference on Metaverse (METAVERSE 2022), the International Conference on Internet of Things (ICIOT 2022), the International Conference on Cognitive Computing (ICCC 2022), the International Conference on Edge Computing (EDGE 2022), and the International Conference on Blockchain (ICBC 2022).

This volume presents the papers accepted at ICCC 2022. Its major topics included Cognitive Computing Technologies and Infrastructure, Cognitive Computing Applications, Sensing Intelligence, Cognitive Analysis, Mobile Services, Cognitive Computing for Smart Homes, and Cognitive Computing for Smart Cities.

We accepted 8 papers, including 6 full papers and 2 short papers. Each was reviewed and selected by three independent members of the ICCC 2022 International Program Committee. We are pleased to thank the authors whose submissions and participation made this conference possible. We also want to express our thanks to the Program Committee members for their dedication in helping to organize the conference and review the submissions.

December 2022

Yujiu Yang
Xiaohui Wang
Liang-Jie Zhang

Organization

Services Conference Federation (SCF 2022)

General Chairs

Ali Arsanjani   Google, USA
Wu Chou   Essenlix, USA

Coordinating Program Chair

Liang-Jie Zhang   Kingdee International Software Group, China

CFO and International Affairs Chair

Min Luo   Georgia Tech, USA

Operations Committee

Jing Zeng   China Gridcom, China
Yishuang Ning   Tsinghua University, China
Sheng He   Tsinghua University, China

Steering Committee

Calton Pu   Georgia Tech, USA
Liang-Jie Zhang   Kingdee International Software Group, China

ICCC 2022

Program Chairs

Yujiu Yang   Tsinghua University, China
Xiaohui Wang   University of Science and Technology Beijing,
                                     China

Program Committee

Yi Zhou   University of Science and Technology Beijing,
                                     China
Liuqing Chen   Zhejiang University, China
Yong Lu   Minzu University, China

Dong Wen	University of Science and Technology Beijing, China
Min Lu	Shenzhen University, China
Ye Liu	University of Chinese Academy of Sciences, China
Peng Xu	Northeast Normal University, China
M. Emre Gursoy	Koc University, Turkey
Carson Leung	University of Manitoba, Canada
Jing Zeng	China Gridcom, China

Services Society

The Services Society (S2) is a non-profit professional organization that was created to promote worldwide research and technical collaboration in services innovations among academia and industrial professionals. Its members are volunteers from industry and academia with common interests. S2 is registered in the USA as a "501(c) organization", which means that it is an American tax-exempt nonprofit organization. S2 collaborates with other professional organizations to sponsor or co-sponsor conferences and to promote an effective services curriculum in colleges and universities. S2 initiates and promotes a "Services University" program worldwide to bridge the gap between industrial needs and university instruction.

The Services Society has formed Special Interest Groups (SIGs) to support technology- and domain-specific professional activities:

- Special Interest Group on Web Services (SIG-WS)
- Special Interest Group on Services Computing (SIG-SC)
- Special Interest Group on Services Industry (SIG-SI)
- Special Interest Group on Big Data (SIG-BD)
- Special Interest Group on Cloud Computing (SIG-CLOUD)
- Special Interest Group on Artificial Intelligence (SIG-AI)
- Special Interest Group on Edge Computing (SIG-EC)
- Special Interest Group on Cognitive Computing (SIG-CC)
- Special Interest Group on Blockchain (SIG-BC)
- Special Interest Group on Internet of Things (SIG-IOT)
- Special Interest Group on Metaverse (SIG-Metaverse)

Services Conference Federation (SCF)

As the founding member of SCF, the first International Conference on Web Services (ICWS) was held in June 2003 in Las Vegas, USA. The First International Conference on Web Services - Europe 2003 (ICWS-Europe'03) was held in Germany in October 2003. ICWS-Europe'03 was an extended event of the 2003 International Conference on Web Services (ICWS 2003) in Europe. In 2004 ICWS-Europe changed to the European Conference on Web Services (ECOWS), which was held in Erfurt, Germany.

SCF 2019 was held successfully during June 25–30, 2019 in San Diego, USA. Affected by COVID-19, SCF 2020 was held online successfully during September 18–20, 2020, and SCF 2021 was held virtually during December 10–14, 2021.

Celebrating its 20-year birthday, the 2022 Services Conference Federation (SCF 2022, http://www.icws.org) was a hybrid conference with a physical onsite in Honolulu, Hawaii, USA, satellite sessions in Shenzhen, Guangdong, China, and also online sessions for those who could not attend onsite. All virtual conference presentations were given via prerecorded videos in December 10–14, 2022 through the BigMarker Video Broadcasting Platform: https://www.bigmarker.com/series/services-conference-federati/series_summit.

Just like SCF 2022, SCF 2023 will most likely be a hybrid conference with physical onsite and virtual sessions online, it will be held in September 2023.

To present a new format and to improve the impact of the conference, we are also planning an Automatic Webinar which will be presented by experts in various fields. All the invited talks will be given via prerecorded videos and will be broadcast in a live-like format recursively by two session channels during the conference period. Each invited talk will be converted into an on-demand webinar right after the conference.

In the past 19 years, the ICWS community has expanded from Web engineering innovations to scientific research for the whole services industry. Service delivery platforms have been expanded to mobile platforms, the Internet of Things, cloud computing, and edge computing. The services ecosystem has been enabled gradually, with value added and intelligence embedded through enabling technologies such as Big Data, artificial intelligence, and cognitive computing. In the coming years, all transactions involving multiple parties will be transformed to blockchain.

Based on technology trends and best practices in the field, the Services Conference Federation (SCF) will continue to serve as a forum for all services-related conferences. SCF 2022 defined the future of the new ABCDE (AI, Blockchain, Cloud, Big Data & IOT). We are very proud to announce that SCF 2023's 10 colocated theme topic conferences will all center around "services", while each will focus on exploring different themes (Web-based services, cloud-based services, Big Data-based services, services innovation lifecycles, AI-driven ubiquitous services, blockchain-driven trust service ecosystems, Metaverse services and applications, and emerging service-oriented technologies).

The 10 colocated SCF 2023 conferences will be sponsored by the Services Society, the world-leading not-for-profit organization dedicated to serving more than 30,000 services computing researchers and practitioners worldwide. A bigger platform means bigger opportunities for all volunteers, authors, and participants. Meanwhile, Springer will provide sponsorship for Best Paper Awards. All 10 conference proceedings of SCF 2023 will be published by Springer, and to date the SCF proceedings have been indexed in the ISI Conference Proceedings Citation Index (included in the Web of Science), the Engineering Index EI (Compendex and Inspec databases), DBLP, Google Scholar, IO-Port, MathSciNet, Scopus, and ZbMath.

SCF 2023 will continue to leverage the invented Conference Blockchain Model (CBM) to innovate the organizing practices for all 10 conferences. Senior researchers in the field are welcome to submit proposals to serve as CBM ambassadors for individual conferences.

SCF 2023 Events

The 2023 edition of the Services Conference Federation (SCF) will include 10 service-oriented conferences: ICWS, CLOUD, SCC, BigData Congress, AIMS, METAVERSE, ICIOT, EDGE, ICCC and ICBC.

The 2023 International Conference on Web Services (ICWS 2023, http://icws.org/2023) will be the flagship theme-topic conference for Web-centric services, enabling technologies and applications.

The 2023 International Conference on Cloud Computing (CLOUD 2023, http://thecloudcomputing.org/2023) will be the flagship theme-topic conference for resource sharing, utility-like usage models, IaaS, PaaS, and SaaS.

The 2023 International Conference on Big Data (BigData 2023, http://bigdatacongress.org/2023) will be the theme-topic conference for data sourcing, data processing, data analysis, data-driven decision-making, and data-centric applications.

The 2023 International Conference on Services Computing (SCC 2023, http://thescc.org/2023) will be the flagship theme-topic conference for leveraging the latest computing technologies to design, develop, deploy, operate, manage, modernize, and redesign business services.

The 2023 International Conference on AI & Mobile Services (AIMS 2023, http://ai1000.org/2023) will be a theme-topic conference for artificial intelligence, neural networks, machine learning, training data sets, AI scenarios, AI delivery channels, and AI supporting infrastructures, as well as mobile Internet services. AIMS will bring AI to mobile devices and other channels.

The 2023 International Conference on Metaverse (Metaverse 2023, http://www.metaverse1000.org/2023) will focus on innovations of the services industry, including financial services, education services, transportation services, energy services, government services, manufacturing services, consulting services, and other industry services.

The 2023 International Conference on Cognitive Computing (ICCC 2023, http://thecognitivecomputing.org/2023) will focus on leveraging the latest computing technologies to simulate, model, implement, and realize cognitive sensing and brain operating systems.

The 2023 International Conference on Internet of Things (ICIOT 2023, http://iciot.org/2023) will focus on the science, technology, and applications of IOT device innovations as well as IOT services in various solution scenarios.

The 2023 International Conference on Edge Computing (EDGE 2023, http://the edgecomputing.org/2023) will be a theme-topic conference for leveraging the latest computing technologies to enable localized device connections, edge gateways, edge applications, edge-cloud interactions, edge-user experiences, and edge business models.

The 2023 International Conference on Blockchain (ICBC 2023, http://blockc hain1000.org/2023) will concentrate on all aspects of blockchain, including digital currencies, distributed application development, industry-specific blockchains, public blockchains, community blockchains, private blockchains, blockchain-based services, and enabling technologies.

Contents

Research Track

Path Planning for Mobile Robots Based on Improved Ant Colony Algorithm

Jie Zhang$^{(\boxtimes)}$ and Xiuqin Pan

School of Information Engineering, Minzu University of China, Beijing 100081, China
20301813@muc.edu.cn

Abstract. In a two-dimensional environment, the traditional ant colony algorithm path planning is prone to problems, such as many turning points, easily falling into a local minimum, and the path is not smooth. To address these problems, a new improved ant colony algorithm is proposed to improve the path optimization performance. First, according to the position of the current grid relative to the start point and the end point, a non-uniform initial pheromone strategy is proposed, so that the closer the dominant grid is, the higher the pheromone concentration is, avoiding blind search by ants and reducing invalid search, and then the introduction of an angular guidance factor to increase the guidance to the end point and to avoid the probability of path zigzagging due to small differences in adjacent grid pheromones, next the pheromone update strategy with a reward and punishment mechanism, the enhancement and decay factors are introduced to adjust the pheromone values adaptively to improve the convergence of the algorithm, final the improved ant colony algorithm and genetic algorithm are fused, and the path is smoothed using the piecewise B-spline curve strategy. The experimental results show that the improved algorithm has greatly improved both the optimization finding ability and the convergence ability.

Keywords: Path planning · Ant colony algorithm · Non-uniform pheromone · Angular guidance factor · Reward and punishment mechanism · Enhancement factors · Decay factors · Genetic algorithm · Piecewise B-spline curve

1 Introduction

Path planning [1] refers to planning a collision-free safe optimal from the start point to the end point in an environment with obstacles. The path has the characteristics of a short walking path and few turning points. Many fruitful path planning algorithms have been proposed by domestic and foreign scholars, such as the A* algorithm [2], artificial potential field method [3], genetic algorithm [4], fuzzy logic algorithm [5], particle swarm algorithm [6], ant colony algorithm [7], deep reinforcement learning [8].

The ant colony algorithm has been widely paid attention to and achieved good results in mobile robot path planning because of its self-organization, positive feedback, parallel computing, and good robustness. Nonetheless, the ant colony algorithm is relatively stochastic, prone to many turn paths, slow convergence of the search path, non-optimal and other problems. Many experts and scholars have proposed relevant optimization strategies for these problems. [9] improved the state transition strategy to improve the convergence speed. Nonetheless, the pheromone distribution in the initial state was uniform, and the ants were blind to search. [10] designed an enhanced ant colony algorithm with a communication mechanism, nonetheless, it took a long time to process information. [11] used pseudo-random state transition rules to select paths, and the optimal and worst solutions were introduced to improve the global pheromone update method. [12] proposed an algorithm combining APF and ACO. The inflection point optimization algorithm was used to reduce the number and length of inflection points in the path, and the curve fitting algorithm was used to optimize the path. Nonetheless, it increased the complexity of the algorithm. [13] improved the path and increased the convergence speed of the algorithm by designing a distance factor and a smoothing factor. [14] initialized the pheromone through the IA algorithm, updated the pheromone using the elite ant colony algorithm, and designed a polynomial smoothing algorithm to smooth the path. [15] designed a group of solutions generated by the Genetic Algorithm, and the solutions were conducted as the initial pheromone of the Ant Colony Algorithm. Then a convergence speed parameter was used to combine the Genetic Algorithm and the Ant Colony Algorithm adaptively. It improved the convergence speed and the local optimum problem. Nonetheless, the global property of the algorithm was reduced.

In this paper, a new improved ant colony algorithm is proposed. Firstly, the initial pheromone non-uniformization strategy is designed based on the idea of the A* algorithm heuristic function, which gives certain directional guidance to the ants in the early stages of the algorithm and reduces invalid searches. Secondly, based on the idea of the artificial potential field method, the angle guidance factor is added to the state transition probability to increase the guidance ability to the end point, speed up the convergence speed of the optimal solution, and reduce the probability of path curvature. Next, the pheromone update strategy with a reward and punishment mechanism is adopted in the pheromone update to make full use of the optimal and worst paths from each iteration of the algorithm, the enhancement and decay factors are introduced to adjust the pheromone values adaptively to improve the convergence of the algorithm. Finally, the improved ant colony algorithm is fused with a genetic algorithm and smoothed using the B-spline curve strategy, avoiding algorithms falling into local minimums and enhancing the stability and generality of algorithms.

2 Original Ant Colony Algorithm

The original ant colony algorithm uses a state transfer formula for path selection, which is given by

$$p_{ij}^m(t) = \begin{cases} \dfrac{\tau_{ij}^{\alpha}(t)\eta_{ij}^{\beta}(t)}{\sum\limits_{s \in \text{allowed}_m} \tau_{ij}^{\alpha}(t)\eta_{ij}^{\beta}(t)} & j \in \text{allowed}_m \\ 0 & \text{else} \end{cases} \quad (1)$$

where i and j are the start point and end point, $\tau_{ij}(t)$ is the pheromone concentration from i to j at moment t; $\eta_{ij}(t)$ is the value of the heuristic function of ant m at node i to j at moment t, the pheromone factor α is the exponent of the pheromone concentration and the heuristic function factor β is the exponent of the heuristic function, and allowed$_m$ is the set of nodes that has not been visited yet.

In the ant colony algorithm, the ant will release pheromones to mark the path it has walked, the pheromone is constantly updated, and the update formula is

$$\tau_{ij}(t+1) = (1-\rho)\tau_{ij}(t) + \sum_{m=1}^{M} \Delta\tau_{ij}^m(t) \tag{2}$$

$$\Delta\tau_{ij}^m = \begin{cases} \dfrac{Q}{L_m}, & \text{if ant m goes through the path node i and j} \\ 0, \text{else} \end{cases} \tag{3}$$

where $\tau_{ij}(t+1)$ is the pheromone concentration on the path of (i, j) at moment t+1, ρ is the pheromone volatility coefficient, M is the total number of ants, Lm is the length of the path walked by ant m, Q is the pheromone increment.

3 Improved Ant Colony Algorithm

3.1 Initial Pheromone Non-uniform Distribution Strategy

The initial pheromone distribution in the original ant colony algorithm is uniform and has a constant value, which makes the ants choose the forward direction with strong randomness and fall into a blind search state, and the convergence speed is slow. To address this problem, we cite the non-uniform initial pheromone strategy in the [16], which is improved to set the following differentiation formula.

$$\tau_i(0) = c^* \frac{d_{se}}{e^*(d_{is}) + (1-e)^*d_{ie}} \tag{4}$$

where $\tau_i(0)$ is the pheromone value of point i in the initial state, dse is the distance from the start point to the end point, d_{is} is the distance from the current point to the start point, d_{ie} is the distance from the current point to the end point, c is the total pheromone control factor, and e is the distance control factor.

Where the value of e ranges from 0 to 1, we set e to a smaller value, which makes it more biased to use die as an evaluation indicator when non-uniformizing the initial pheromone, further increasing the attractiveness of the end point and speeding up the convergence of the solution. This method non-uniformizes the initial pheromone so that the concentration of pheromone values is greatest in the region near the line connecting the start point and end point. The further away from the line, the lower the pheromone concentration. The high pheromone concentration gives the initial ants some directional guidance, and makes them avoid blind search and reduce the invalid search. Therefore, we can accelerate the convergence speed of the algorithm, and improve the quality of the obtained solution.

3.2 State Transfer Formula Improvement Strategy

In the original ant colony algorithm, the distance between the points of neighboring grids is not significantly different, so it is difficult for the ants to make a correct choice, which leads to a high zigzag rate of the searched path and low search efficiency. The introduction of the angle guidance factor can effectively increase the ant's ability to guide the end point and make the ant move in a better direction, thus improving the quality of the solution, reducing the probability of zigzagging, and improving the search speed. The calculation method is shown as follows.

$$\cos\theta_{ij} = \frac{(j_x - i_x) * (E_x - i_x) + (j_y - i_y) * (E_y - i_y)}{\sqrt{(j_x - i_x)^2 + (j_y - i_y)^2}\sqrt{(E_x - i_x)^2 + (E_y - i_y)^2}} \tag{5}$$

$$\theta_{ij} = \arccos\theta_{ij} \tag{6}$$

$$v_{ij} = \frac{180 - \theta_{ij}}{180 + \theta_{ij}} \tag{7}$$

where i is the current grid, j is the next grid, E is the end point grid, and the coordinates of the current node are (i_x, i_y), the next node coordinates are (j_x, j_y), and the coordinates of the end point are (E_x, E_y), $\theta_{ij} = \angle jiE$ is the angle of the angle factor, whose range is $[0, 180°]$. Based on the inverse cosine function to calculate the θ_{ij}, as the angle factor is too large to affect the transfer probability calculation, we normalize it as shown in the formula (7). The angle guidance factor gradually decreases to 0 as the angle increases, and when its value is closer to 1, it means that the next direction of the ant is closer to the ideal search direction, and the search effect is better. The improved transfer probability is shown as follows.

$$p_{ij}^m(t) = \begin{cases} \dfrac{\tau_{ij}^\alpha(t)\eta_{ij}^\beta(t)v_{ij}^r(t)}{\sum\limits_{s\in allowed_m} \tau_{ij}^\alpha(t)\eta_{ij}^\beta(t)v_{ij}^r(t)} & j \in allowed_m \\ 0 \; else \end{cases} \tag{8}$$

where the original ant colony related parameters are unchanged and $v_{ij}(t)$ is the angular guidance factor at moment t, r is its importance.

3.3 Pheromone Update Strategy

In this paper, a pheromone reward and punishment strategy is introduced by adding some additional pheromones to the optimal paths generated by each iteration and decreasing some additional pheromones for the worst path produced by each iteration. Although the proposed strategy can enhance the guidance of subsequent ants, the probability of falling into a local optimum is increased in the long run. To address this problem, the enhancement factor was proposed by [17], and they designed the decay factor w to adjust the pheromone values adaptively, which is calculated as shown below.

$$\tau_{ij}(t+1) = (1-\rho)\tau_{ij}(t) + \sum_{m=1}^{M}\Delta\tau_{ij}^m(t) + q\Delta\tau_{best}^N(t) - w\Delta\tau_{worst}^N(t) \tag{9}$$

$$q = e^{\frac{N-1}{N_{max}}} - 1 \qquad (10)$$

$$w = e^{\frac{N_{max}-N+1}{N_{max}+N-1}-1} \qquad (11)$$

where N is the current number of iterations, N_{max} is the maximum number of iterations. The enhancement factor q increases with the number of iterations increases. To ensure the diversity of solutions, in the early iterations of the algorithm, the enhancement factor q is approximately 0, the optimal solution is almost never enhanced, and in the later iterations of the algorithm, the paths do not differ much. To avoid different paths having approximately the same pheromone concentration, additional pheromone was added only when a new optimal solution appeared, so that the pheromone concentration of the current optimal path quickly surpasses the pheromone concentration of the historical path, avoiding the algorithm falling into local convergence. The decay factor w decreases with the number of iterations increases, and the probability of searching for the worst path is the largest in the early stage of the algorithm, thus making the value of the decay factor w larger. Later, the pheromone distribution gradually tends to mature, and the pheromone of a node on the worst path may also exert an impact on the optimal path, so a small fraction of the pheromone of the worst path was preserved to speed up the convergence of the algorithm and avoid the algorithm falling into a local optimum.

3.4 Ant Colony and Genetic Algorithm Fusion Strategy

Genetic Algorithm (GA) is a stochastic global search and optimization method developed by simulating biological evolutionary mechanisms, which draws on Darwinian evolution and Mendelian genetic theory.

A fitness function is used for path selection in the genetic algorithm, which is formulated as

$$\text{fit} = w_1 \text{fit}_1 + w_2 \text{fit}_2 \qquad (12)$$

$$\text{fit}_1 = \frac{1}{\sum_{i=1}^{end-1} \sqrt{(x_{i+1} - x_i)^2 + (y_{i+1} - y_i)^2}} \qquad (13)$$

$$\text{fit}_2 = \frac{1}{\lambda + \arccos\left(\frac{b^2 + c^2 - a^2}{2bc}\right)} \qquad (14)$$

The fitness function is divided into two parts, which are used to determine the length of the path and the degree of smoothing. fit_1 denotes the inverse of the total length of the path, fit_2 is the inverse of the size of the angle formed by the adjacent three points by the inverse cosine function. Given a penalty of λ, the smoother the path, the greater the angle formed by the adjacent three points. The smoothness is best if the three points form a line, followed by obtuse, right, and acute angles. The three cases were given different penalties except for straight lines, λ is 500 in obtuse angles, λ is 20 in right angles, and λ is 4 in obtuse angles. The parameters w_1 and w_2 are selected according to the weights of both path length and smoothness.

The traditional ant colony algorithm and genetic algorithms have many shortcomings in the application of mobile robot path planning. The path planning optimization effect is not very satisfactory. To address the shortcomings of the two algorithms, this paper fuses the two algorithms with the advantages of each. Based on the ant colony algorithm, the initial population of the genetic algorithm is no longer randomly generated. Rather, the optimal path generated by the ant colony algorithm is used as the initial population, and through continuous selection, crossover, and mutation to produce more individuals with higher adaptability as excellent individuals. The fusion of the two algorithms can greatly enhance the stability and generality of the algorithm.

3.5 Piecewise B-Spline Curve Smoothing Strategy

In this paper, the piecewise B-spline curves were used to make the road flat around the inflection point.

$$P(t) = \sum_{i=0}^{n} B_{i,k}(t)p_i \tag{15}$$

$$B_{i,0}(t) = \begin{cases} 1, t_i \leq t \leq t_{i+1} \\ 0, \text{ otherwise} \end{cases} \tag{16}$$

$$B_{i,k}(t) = \frac{(t - t_i)B_{i,k-1}(t)}{t_{i+k} - t_i} + \frac{(t_{i+k+1} - t)B_{i+1,k-1}(t)}{t_{i+k+1} - t_{i+1}} \tag{17}$$

A B-spline curve is defined by $n + 1$ control points p_i and a knot vector t, where $B_{i,k}(u)$ is the B-spline based function defined by the DeBoor-Cox recursion formulas (16) and (17).

This paper's piecewise B-spline curve strategy is to interpolate the route first, only needing to find the three points that need to be smoothed the turn for B-spline processing, and the combination of the smoothed points and the interpolated processed points, so as to reach the smooth path. Based on this method, it can not only meet the requirement of modifying the local path when planning the path without changing the whole path shape but also complete the post-fitting of the path points to generate smooth paths.

The following is a diagram of the smooth path of the piecewise B-spline curve (Fig. 1).

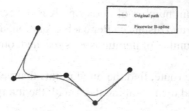

Fig. 1. Schematic diagram of the smooth path of the piecewise B-spline curve

4 The Execution Steps of the Improved Algorithm

Step 1. Create the grid map 0–1 matrix, determine the start point and end point; initialize the parameters: number of ant colony iterations N_{max}, number of ants M, pheromone factor α, heuristic factor β, pheromone volatility factor ρ, pheromone initial value τ_0, pheromone intensity Q, etc.

Step 2. The initial pheromone is non-uniformized using a weighted pheromone assignment strategy, and the initial value $\tau_i(0)$ of the pheromone for each grid is calculated according to the formula.

Step 3. Place M ants at the start point, initialize the taboo table, the set of path points, and the path length. Add the start point to the taboo table and calculate the angle guidance factor according to the formula.

Step 4. Calculate the state transfer probability of the next feasible grid according to the formula, select the next grid using the roulette method, and update the forbidden table of this ant.

Step 5. Determine if the ant has reached the end point. If not, return to execute steps 3 and 4, otherwise, execute step 6.

Step 6. When all ants have searched in each iteration, the pheromone update strategy with a reward and punishment mechanism is used to update the pheromones of all paths that have successfully reached the end point.

Step 7. If the maximum number of iterations is not reached N_{max} then execute steps 3 to 7 again, keeping all the iterations of the routes walked by ants in each iteration and adding 1 to the number of iterations; if the maximum number of iterations is reached N_{max}, sort the routes according to the distance from smallest to largest.

Step 8. Initialize the population and each path's fitness function value, average path, minimum path, maximum evolution number K of the genetic algorithm, crossover probability, and mutation probability.

Step 9. The sum of the fitness functions of all individuals is calculated, and then the ratio of each individual is calculated, and the better individual retained is selected using the roulette wheel method.

Step 10. If the crossover probability is reached, find all the same points in the paths of the two paths, select one of the points at random, and crossover the paths after this point.

Step 11. If the mutation probability is reached, two grids are randomly selected except for the start point and end point, the path between the selected points is deleted, and the two points are processed consecutively again until the mutation operation is completed.

Step 12. If the maximum number of iterations K is not reached, execute steps 9 to 12 again, keeping the route and distance after each evolution, and add 1 to the evolution number; if the maximum number of iterations K is reached, output the optimal path and iteration curve.

Step 13. Interpolate the route, find the three points that need to make smooth turns for B-spline processing, and then combine them with the interpolated points.

5   Simulation Experiment and Analysis

The performance of this paper's algorithm is verified by simulation experiments related to two maps of 20×20 and 30×30. To minimize the influence of the simulation parameters on the experimental results, we went through several experimental verifications and finally selected the simulation parameters as follows. N_{max} is 100, M is 50, α is 2, β is 6, r is 4, ρ is 0.1, Q is 1, a = 1, c = 1, e = 0.2, K is 200, the crossover probability is 0.2, and the mutation probability is 0.05 (Figs. 2 and 3).

5.1   20 × 20 Grid Map Simulation Experiments

The original ant colony algorithm, the improved ant colony algorithm, the original ant colony and genetic fusion algorithm, and the improved ant colony and genetic fusion algorithm were simulated using a grid map with a specification of 20×20, and the data comparison table is shown in Table 1.

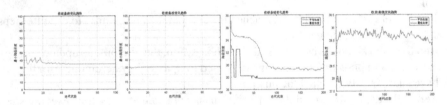

Fig. 2. Comparison of convergence curve changes of four algorithms

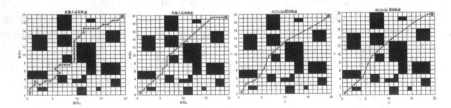

Fig. 3. Comparison chart of robot motion trajectory changes of four algorithms

In Table 1, it can be seen that the path length of the improved ant colony algorithm is reduced from 34.3848 to 28.6274, the number of convergence iterations is reduced from 20 to 10, and the number of turning points is reduced from 29 to 22. By fusing the

Table 1. Comparison of experimental results.

Algorithm evaluation metrics	ACO	IACO	ACO + GA	IACO + GA
Path convergence length	34.3848	28.6274	27.7923	27.7207
Number of iterations convergence	20	10	60	10
Number of turning points	29	22	13	13

original ant colony algorithm with the genetic algorithm in this paper, the complexity of the algorithm and the number of iterations increase, which makes the convergence speed slower, but there is a great improvement in the path length and smoothness, which verifies the effectiveness of the genetic algorithm. The improved ant colony algorithm is fused with the genetic algorithm, the fused algorithm is improved in terms of path length and number of iterations, which further verifies the effectiveness of the algorithm in this paper (Figs. 4 and 5).

5.2   30 × 30 Grid Map Simulation Experiments

The original ant colony algorithm, the improved ant colony algorithm, the original ant colony and genetic fusion algorithm, and the improved ant colony and genetic fusion algorithm were simulated using a grid map with a specification of 30 × 30, and the data comparison table is shown in Table 2.

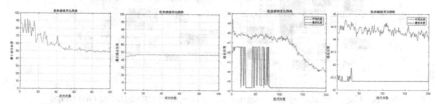

Fig. 4. Comparison of convergence curve changes of four algorithms

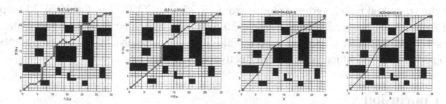

Fig. 5. Comparison chart of robot motion trajectory changes of four algorithms

In Table 2, it can be seen that the route length of the improved ant colony algorithm is reduced from 48.2843 to 44.5269, the number of convergence iterations is reduced from 50 to 10, and the number of turning points is reduced from 40 to 35. By fusing the original ant colony algorithm with the genetic algorithm in this paper, the complexity

Table 2. Comparison of experimental results.

Algorithm evaluation metrics	ACO	IACO	ACO + GA	IACO + GA
Path convergence length	48.2843	44.5269	42.3660	42.3522
Number of iterations convergence	50	10	75	25
Number of turning points	40	35	11	10

of the algorithm and the number of iterations increase, which makes the convergence speed slower, but there is a great improvement in the path length and smoothness, which verifies the effectiveness of the genetic algorithm. The improved ant colony algorithm is fused with the genetic algorithm, although the number of iterations increases and the complexity of the algorithm becomes higher compared with the improved original ant colony algorithm, it is improved in all aspects compared with the original ant colony and genetic fusion algorithm, which further verifies the effectiveness of the algorithm in this paper.

5.3 Optimal Path Smoothing Experiment

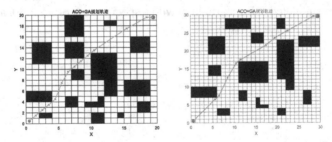

Fig. 6. The path after smoothing with the B-spline curve under two maps

The optimal paths obtained from the two maps are smoothed using B-spline curves, and the smoothed path length is reduced from 27.7207 to 27.7027 in the 20×20 map and from 42.3522 to 42.3349 in the 30×30 map, and as can be seen from the figure, the smoothed paths are tangent to the original paths, the paths around the turning points also become flatter, which verifies the effectiveness of the algorithm Fig. 6.

6   Conclusion

For the original ant colony algorithm path planning has many turning points, easy to fall into a local optimum, and the path is not smooth enough. A new improved ant colony algorithm is proposed. Firstly, the initial pheromone non-uniform strategy is designed to improve the convergence speed of the algorithm. Secondly, the angle guidance factor is increased to speed up the convergence of the optimal solution and reduce the probability of path curvature. Thirdly, the enhancement factor and decay factor are introduced, and the pheromone update strategy with reward and punishment mechanism is used to adjust the pheromone value adaptively, avoiding the local optimum and improving the convergence of the algorithm. The improved ant colony algorithm is fused with the genetic algorithm and smoothed using the piecewise B-spline curve strategy, which not only solves the problem that the ant colony algorithm easily falls into local optimum, but also greatly enhances the stability and generality of the algorithm. The simulation results show that the optimal path found in this paper requires fewer iterations, shorter paths, fewer turning points, and better performance in finding the optimal path.

References

1. Zhang, S., Pu, J., Si, Y., Sun, L.: Survey on the application of ant colony algorithm in path planning of mobile robot. Comput. Eng. Appl. 56(8), 10–19 (2020)
2. Guruji, A.K., Agarwal, H., Parsediya, D.K.: Time-efficient A* algorithm for robot path planning. Procedia Technol. 23, 144–149 (2016)
3. Wang, P., Gao, S., Li, L., Sun, B., Cheng, S.: Obstacle avoidance path planning design for autonomous driving vehicles based on an improved artificial potential field algorithm. Energies 12(12), 2342 (2019)
4. Ermakov, S.M., Semenchikov, D.N.: Genetic global optimization algorithms. Commun. Stat.-Simul. Comput. 51(4), 1503–1512 (2022)
5. Pradhan, S.K., Parhi, D.R., Panda, A.K.: Fuzzy logic techniques for navigation of several mobile robots. Appl. Soft Comput. 9(1), 290–304 (2009)
6. Li, G., Chou, W.: Path planning for mobile robot using self-adaptive learning particle swarm optimization. Sci. China Inf. Sci. 61(5), 1–18 (2017). https://doi.org/10.1007/s11432-016-9115-2
7. Yang, H., Qi, J., Miao, Y., Sun, H., Li, J.: A new robot navigation algorithm based on a double-layer ant algorithm and trajectory optimization. IEEE Trans. Industr. Electron. 66(11), 8557–8566 (2018)
8. Tai, L., Liu, M.: A robot exploration strategy based on q-learning network. In: 2016 IEEE International Conference on Real-time Computing and Robotics, pp. 57–62. IEEE (2016)
9. Qi, D., Zhang, Z., Zhang, Q.: Path planning of multirotor UAV based on the improved ant colony algorithm. J. Robot. 2022 (2022)
10. Hou, W., Xiong, Z., Wang, C., Chen, H.: Enhanced ant colony algorithm with communication mechanism for mobile robot path planning. Robot. Auton. Syst. 148, 103949 (2022)
11. Zheng, Y., Luo, Q., Wang, H., Wang, C., Chen, X.: Path planning of mobile robot based on adaptive ant colony algorithm. J. Intell. Fuzzy Syst. 39(4), 5329–5338 (2020)
12. Fu, J., Lv, T., Li, B.: Underwater submarine path planning based on artificial potential field ant colony algorithm and velocity obstacle method. Sensors 22(10) (2022)
13. Yang, L., et al.: LF-ACO: an effective formation path planning for multi-mobile robot. Math. Biosci. Eng. 19(1), 225–252 (2022)
14. Wang, H., Zhang, J., Dong, J.: Application of ant colony and immune combined optimization algorithm in path planning of unmanned CRAF. AIP Adv. 12(2), 025313 (2022)
15. Chen, J., et al.: Robot path planning based on adaptive integrating of genetic and ant colony algorithm. Int. J. Innov. Comput. Inf. Control 11(3), 833–850 (2015)
16. Zhang, S., et al.: Path planning for mobile robot using an enhanced ant colony optimization and path geometric optimization. Int. J. Adv. Robot. Syst. 18(3) (2021)
17. Yang, H., Qi, J., Miao, Y., Sun, H., Li, J.: A new robot navigation algorithm based on a double-layer ant algorithm and trajectory optimization. IEEE Trans. Industr. Electron. 66(11), 8557–8566 (2018)

Solving a Cloze Test for Generative Commonsense Question Answering

Xuan Luo, Yihui Li, and Ruifeng Xu$^{(\boxtimes)}$

Harbin Institute of Technology (Shenzhen), Shenzhen, China
gracexluo@hotmail.com, 20S051013@stu.hit.edu.cn, xuruifeng@hit.edu.cn

Abstract. Commonsense question answering has always been a challenging task due to the wide-domain coverage and the implicity of commonsense knowledge. Few works are tackling the answer generation of commonsense questions, which is more difficult than multiple-choice. This motivates us to delve into the answer generation ability of pretrained language models (PLMs). Other than utilizing knowledge bases to extract commonsense-related knowledge to answer commonsense questions, we exploit the latent knowledge within PLMs to solve this task. In this work, we reformulate this generative task into a masked token prediction task and experiment with masked language models (MLMs) and generative language models (GLMs). Experimental results on the ProtoQA dataset demonstrate the effectiveness of our proposed method. Our work finds that both MLMs and GLMs are good at masked token prediction and that PLMs have acquired commonsense knowledge through large-corpus pre-training.

Keyword: Commonsense question answering

1 Introduction

Commonsense reasoning has been put on the agenda since the earliest days of artificial intelligence. Commonsense question answering is one of its applications and it has always been a challenging task. Unlike answering factoid questions, which can be solved by retrieving answers from the text explicitly describing the fact, answering commonsense questions rely on commonsense knowledge which is implicit and spreads in various domain.

Traditionally, commonsense question answering tasks are in the form of multiple-choice, such as CommonsenseQA [14] and SocialIQA [12], where the correct answer is contained in the answer choices provided. However, in real-life scenarios, it is more likely to answer commonsense questions by generating answers than selecting them from candidate answer choices provided. Therefore, answer generation to commonsense questions is more practical. Moreover, there are occasions where the commonsensical answers to commonsense questions are not unique. To fill this gap, Boratko et al. published a novel dataset ProtoQA

Y. Yang et al. (Eds.): ICCC 2022, LNCS 13734, pp. 14–24, 2022.
https://doi.org/10.1007/978-3-031-23585-6_2

in 2020 [1]. It is a benchmark for testing models' ability to commonsense reasoning over prototypical situations where there could be many different answers and some answers are commoner or more typical than others. For instance, in Fig. 1, a prototypical commonsense question "At the beach, name something that might protect you from sun." and its answers with the numbers indicating their typicality. Since it provides no answer choices and context related to the questions, it is more challenging than multiple-choice datasets.

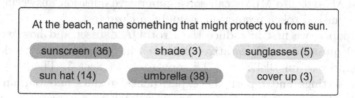

Fig. 1. An example from ProtoQA train set. The answers are collected with the numbers indicating their typicality.

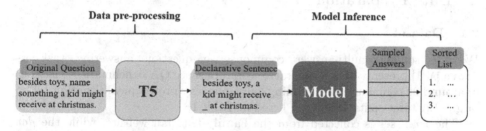

Fig. 2. The framework of solving a cloze test.

Intuitively, generative language models (GLMs) are paradigms for generative tasks and there is nothing to do with masked language models (MLMs) since MLMs are widely used for multiple-choice. What if we change this question to a declarative sentence:

At the beach, [MASK] *might protect you from sun*

where the [MASK] should be replaced by answers, such as *sunscreen*.

The procedure of predicting the tokens of [MASK] is called Masked Token Prediction. This is a part of the pre-training tasks of many PLMs, such as BERT [4] and T5 [11]. In addition, several studies [3,9] have shown that PLMs are implicit sources of world knowledge. According to these, we assume that PLMs pre-trained with masked token prediction can perform commonsense question answering by masked token prediction without extra knowledge bases.

To test our assumption, we utilize T5 with prompt learning to reformulate the generative commonsense answering task into a cloze test, namely, a masked token prediction task. The framework of our method is demonstrated in Fig. 2.

It contains two steps: data pre-processing and model inference. In data pre-processing, the original question is converted into a declarative sentence by the fine-tuned T5. In model inference, the fine-tuned model conduct masked token prediction and then the sampled answers are sorted as final results.

The experimental results on ProtoQA dataset demonstrate the effectiveness of our proposed method and verify our assumption. They also imply that PLMs have acquired commonsense knowledge through large-corpusc which corroborates that PLMs are implicit sources of world knowledge. Our study shows that not only GLMs but also MLMs can solve generative question answering task in the form of masked token prediction, namely, a cloze test.

In this paper, we first introduce the ProtoQA dataset and how we rewrite the original questions to declarative sentences in Sect. 2. Next, we detail our fine-tuning process on BERT and T5 separately in Sect. 3. Then, we list the experiment settings and report the experimental results and our analysis in Sect. 4. After that, we categorize the works related to our research in Sect. 5. Finally, we summarize our work in the conclusion.

2 Data Preparation

2.1 Dataset

We are solving multi-answer commonsense question answering task as ProtoQA [1] presents. It is a generative commonsense QA benchmark, consisting of around 9k commonsense reasoning questions over prototypical situation.[1] The original dataset splits of [1]'s are listed in Table 1.

The *train* set is collected from the Family-feud fan website, while the *dev* set contains newly written questions and answers by crowd-workers, so does the *test* set. The distribution of answers' length is shown in Fig. 3, and the average number of answers for each question in *train* set is 5.

An example is shown in Fig. 1. Each question has several reasonable answers, with the numbers indicating their typicality. All the answers are categorized into non-overlapped clusters and the answers within the same cluster share the same typicality. Models are expected to generate most common answers which should cover various categories as much as possible within the limited number of answers.

Table 1. The statistics of ProtoQA dataset.

Dataset	Train	Dev	Test
ProtoQA	8782	52	102

---

[1] https://github.com/iesl/protoqa-data.

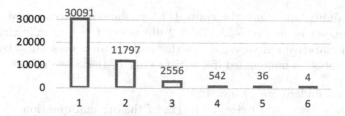

Fig. 3. The distribution of answers' length.

2.2 Declarative Sentences Generation

As shown in Fig. 1, the way of describing a question is suitable for GLMs to generate plausible answers. In order to perform masked token prediction, we utilize T5 to change the original questions into declarative sentences.

First, we train T5 with prompt learning to teach it how to rewrite. The input is as follows:

$$declarative : \parallel question \parallel </s>$$

where $declarative$: is the prompt; $</s>$ is a special token; $question$ is the original question line in the dataset. These three are concatenated as one string. The output is as follows:

$$target \parallel </s>$$

where $target$ is the declarative sentence we expected. For the training of the rewriter T5, the target sentences are rewritten manually, 102 pieces in all. We have selected sentences where answers act as different components to rewrite, so that T5 can learn to write declarative sentences under various situations.

Table 2. Examples of declarative sentences. _ represents [MASK]; **Q** represents the original question; **D** represents the declarative sentence.

Manual
Q: name something that is hard to guess about a person you are just meeting
D: it is hard to guess about the _ of a person you are just meeting
Q: name something a monk probably would not own
D: a monk probably would not own _
Q: name something that people usually do before they leave the house for work?
D: people usually _ before they leave the house for work
Generated
Q: apart from horses, name something you might see at a horse race
D: apart from horses, you might see _ at a horse race
Q: after their parents say no name something kids do to get what they want
D: after their parents say no, kids _ to get what they want
Q: besides toys, name something a kid might receive at christmas
D: besides toys, a kid might receive _ at christmas

After training, we apply the trained T5 to generate declarative sentences for all the questions in ProtoQA. Table 2 illustrates the manually-written and generated declarative sentences, where the underscore represents [MASK]. We regard a sentence as unqualified if it satisfies one of these two conditions:

1) There is no underscore within.
2) Its length is more than twice the length of the original question.

We have 8670 pieces of qualified declarative sentences generated by T5. Worth mentioning, we only got 5118 pieces of qualified declarative sentences when training T5 without prompt.

3   Masked Token Prediction

3.1   BERT

For BERT's training, we first pre-process declarative sentences with answers filled within. Masked declarative sentences are the inputs and the masked tokens are the labels. Here are our rules for masking:

1) Words within answer spans are masked with 0.9 probability.
2) The other words are masked with 0.15 probability

For BERT's inference, since BERT conducts masked token prediction with specified number of [MASK], we create two templates according to Fig. 3:

1) *people usually* [**MASK**] *before they leave the house for work.*
2) *people usually* [**MASK**] [**MASK**] *before they leave the house for work.*

As shown in Fig. 4, the two files with either template are fed into BERT; then, these prediction files are combined to be one list of final results.

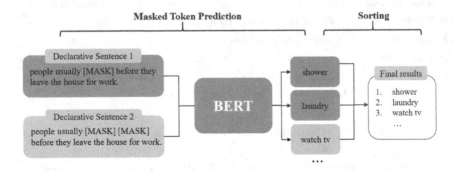

Fig. 4. The workflow of BERT's inference.

3.2   T5

For T5's training, we mask the answer spans of the input sequence with so-called sentinel tokens (a.k.a unique mask tokens) "**<extra_id_0>**" and the output sequence is formed as a concatenation of the same sentinel tokens and the real masked tokens. For instance,

Input: *people usually* **<extra_id_0>** *before they leave the house for work.*
Output 1: **<extra_id_0>** *shower* **<extra_id_1>**
Output 2: **<extra_id_0>** *have breakfast* **<extra_id_1>**
Output 3: **<extra_id_0>** *close the door* **<extra_id_1>**

For T5's inference, since T5 has been trained with the span-mask denoising objective, it can be used to predict the sentinel (masked-out) tokens during inference. The predicted tokens will then be placed between the sentinel tokens. As shown in Fig. 5, the input template is the same as training's and the final results are the sorted predictions by the occurrence of predicted spans.

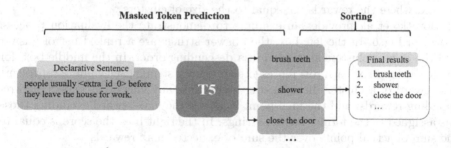

Fig. 5. The workflow of T5's inference.

4   Experiments

4.1   Settings

We use **BERT** and **T5** to do the cloze test. The learning rate scheduler is linear and the optimizer is AdamW. The other settings of training are listed in Table 3. We reimplement the baseline model **GPT-2** proposed by [1], which generates the answers after the question lines, and the setting is listed in Table 3 as well.

Because the test set answers are hidden and we need the ground-truth answers to test our hypothesis, we split the *train* set into two parts for training and validation. We report results on the *dev* set. During inference, following [1]'s setting, we sample 300 times for each question.

Table 3. The settings of training.

Model	Learning Rate	Epoch	Batch Size	Precision
BERT-large-uncased	2e−4	5	32	16
t5-large	1e−4	3	16	32
gpt2-large	1e−5	1	8	16

4.2 Evaluation

We follow the metrics proposed for ProtoQA by [1]:

Max Answers @ k: allows limited total number of answers, up to k answers.
Max Incorrect @ k: allows unlimited answers; stops after k unmatched answers.

Employing the Hungarian matching algorithm [5,8], the metrics compute the optimal matching between the answers and the clusters based on the reward matrix, where the rewards are equal to the size of clusters.[2]

Boratko et al. provides an example to demonstrate the evaluation process, shown in Fig. 6. In the left box, the answer strings are a ranked list of answer and the answer clusters are sorted in a descending order. In the middle box, for the reward matrix, each row represents an answer string; each column represents the reward of a cluster. If an answer string hits any cluster, it gets the corresponding rewards, and the final point it gets is the max reward excluding those has assigned to the former answer strings. In the right box, the score is equal to the sum of actual points over the sum of expected max rewards.

Name something that people usually do before they leave for work.

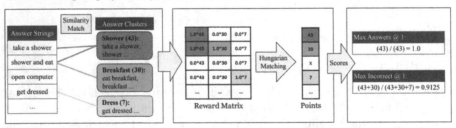

Fig. 6. An example evaluation steps for a ranked list of answers [1].

---

[2] https://github.com/iesl/protoqa-evaluator.

4.3   Main Results

Our methods are **BERT MTP** and **T5 MTP**, where MTP is short for masked token prediction.

We compare our method with four baselines in [1]:

1) Human*.
2) QA Model*: extracting answers from context retrieved from Google.
3) GPT-2*: vanilla gpt2-large for original task form.
4) GPT-2 FT*: fine-tuned gpt2-large for original task form.

Table 4. Main results on the ProtoQA *dev* set. Note that the scores of models with * are reported on the test set by [1], we assume that the scores would be similar on dev set. **GPT-2 FT** is the reimplement on *dev* set.

Model	Max Answers (%)				Max Incorrect (%)		
	@ 1	@ 3	@ 5	@ 10	@ 1	@ 3	@ 5
Human*	78.4	76.8	76.0	77.0	59.0	74.0	77.9
QA Model*	3.4	6.4	9.1	15.7	1.4	5.3	8.4
GPT-2*	6.2	18.5	23.0	30.5	4.3	17.9	24.2
GPT-2 FT*	36.4	44.4	46.4	53.5	26.1	41.7	48.2
GPT-2 FT	41.9	43.2	47.6	52.6	21.7	38.5	49.1
BERT MTP	**46.7**	48.0	**51.1**	52.4	**35.7**	42.3	48.0
T5 MTP	37.6	**48.2**	49.5	**59.6**	25.8	**45.5**	**53.5**

According to Table 4, the best scores all fall in the **MTP** lines and these two models are superior than the baselines overall, which demonstrate the effectiveness of our method. Compared with T5, BERT has its advantage on metrics Max Answer @ 1 and Max Incorrect @ 1, while falls behind T5 when predicting more plausible answers.

4.4   Ablation Study

For ablation study, we compare with the following models:

1) BERT FT: fine-tuned bert-large-uncased for original task form; specifically, [MASK]s are placed at the end of the question lines.
2) T5 FT: fine-tuned t5-large for original task form.
3) BERT: vanilla bert-large-uncased for masked token prediction.
4) T5: vanilla t5-large for masked token prediction.

According Table 5, T5 and GPT-2 are comparative under the original task form while BERT is much inferior. This phenomenon may be explained by the characters of models. BERT is a bi-directional encoder, which is well-known for

Table 5. The results of ablation study on the ProtoQA *dev* set. The first section are models fine-tuned with the original task form. The other sections are models performing the masked token prediction task.

Model	Max Answers (%)				Max Incorrect (%)		
	@ 1	@ 3	@ 5	@ 10	@ 1	@ 3	@ 5
GPT-2*	6.2	18.5	23.0	30.5	4.3	17.9	24.2
GPT-2 FT*	36.4	44.4	46.4	53.5	26.1	41.7	48.2
GPT-2 FT	41.9	43.2	47.6	52.6	21.7	38.5	49.1
BERT FT	23.5	34.5	37.1	36.0	15.0	29.3	34.4
T5 FT	36.1	40.0	45.2	54.3	23.5	37.7	47.2
BERT	10.0	14.5	13.7	17.5	5.0	11.8	13.1
BERT MTP	**46.7**	48.0	**51.1**	52.4	**35.7**	42.3	48.0
T5	0.0	0.0	0.4	1.1	0.0	0.0	0.4
T5 MTP	37.6	**48.2**	49.5	**59.6**	25.8	**45.5**	**53.5**

take advantage of information from both directions. T5 and GPT-2 are unidirectional decoders whose design are more proper to the task form.

For the masked token prediction task, on one hand, vanilla BERT model performs much better than T5, which is again consistent with the characters mentioned above. On the other hand, T5 has greater improvement after fine tuning on masked token prediction than BERT. This may because T5 is more knowledgeable or better at learning.

5   Related Works

The advent of pre-trained language models (PLMs) brings an ever increasing zeal for commonsense reasoning research. These powerful PLMs are roughly categorized into masked language models (MLMs) and generative language models (GLMs). MLMs, such as BERT [4], are famous for classification tasks. GLMs, such as GPT-2 [10], perform well on generation tasks. T5 [11], a unified text-to-text transformer, is good at both classification and generation tasks with proper prompt during both training and inference.

On one hand, previous works evaluated LMs against commonsense benchmarks to probe the commonsense knowledge learned by LMs. On the other hand, recent studies have shown that PLMs are implicit sources of world knowledge [3,9]. Based on the observation of recent studies, we put forward our method with the assumption that PLMs have acquire commonsense knowledge. Therefore, we exploit PLMs instead of utilizing external knowledge.

There are few works experimenting on ProtoQA dataset. [7] studied the effect of fine-tuning and prompt methods [6,13] on PLM's learning process and [2] compared the quality of the distributions generated by different LMs for answering ambiguous questions. We utilize this dataset to solve a multi-answer generation task by masked token prediction.

6   Conclusion

We propose to solve a generative commonsense question answering task as a cloze test. We reformulate the generative task to a masked token prediction task and experiment with both masked language model and generative language model. The experimental results demonstrate that our method is effectiveness and that the generative question answering task can be solved by both masked language models and generative language models.

Acknowledgement. This work was partially supported by the National Natural Science Foundation of China (62006062, 62176076), Shenzhen Key Technology Project JSGG20210802154400001.

References

1. Boratko, M., Li, X., O'Gorman, T., Das, R., Le, D., McCallum, A.: ProtoQA: A question answering dataset for prototypical common-sense reasoning. In: Proceedings of the 2020 Conference on Empirical Methods in Natural Language Processing (EMNLP), pp. 1122–1136. Association for Computational Linguistics, Online, November 2020. https://aclanthology.org/2020.emnlp-main.85
2. Chang, H.S., McCallum, A.: Softmax bottleneck makes language models unable to represent multi-mode word distributions. In: Proceedings of the 60th Annual Meeting of the Association for Computational Linguistics (Volume 1: Long Papers), pp. 8048–8073. Association for Computational Linguistics, Dublin, Ireland, May 2022. https://aclanthology.org/2022.acl-long.554
3. Davison, J., Feldman, J., Rush, A.: Commonsense knowledge mining from pre-trained models. In: Proceedings of the 2019 Conference on Empirical Methods in Natural Language Processing and the 9th International Joint Conference on Natural Language Processing (EMNLP-IJCNLP), pp. 1173–1178. Association for Computational Linguistics, Hong Kong, China, November 2019. https://aclanthology.org/D19-1109
4. Devlin, J., Chang, M.W., Lee, K., Toutanova, K.: Bert: Pre-training of deep bidirectional transformers for language understanding. In: Proceedings of the 2019 Conference of the North American Chapter of the Association for Computational Linguistics: Human Language Technologies, Volume 1 (Long and Short Papers), pp. 4171–4186 (2019)
5. Kuhn, H.W.: The hungarian method for the assignment problem. Naval Res. Logist. Quart. **2**(1–2), 83–97 (1955)
6. Li, X.L., Liang, P.: Prefix-tuning: optimizing continuous prompts for generation. In: Proceedings of the 59th Annual Meeting of the Association for Computational Linguistics and the 11th International Joint Conference on Natural Language Processing (Volume 1: Long Papers), pp. 4582–4597. Association for Computational Linguistics, Online, August 2021. https://aclanthology.org/2021.acl-long.353
7. Ma, K., Ilievski, F., Francis, J., Ozaki, S., Nyberg, E., Oltramari, A.: Exploring strategies for generalizable commonsense reasoning with pre-trained models. In: Proceedings of the 2021 Conference on Empirical Methods in Natural Language Processing, pp. 5474–5483. Association for Computational Linguistics, Online and Punta Cana, Dominican Republic, November 2021. https://aclanthology.org/2021.emnlp-main.445

8. Munkres, J.: Algorithms for the assignment and transportation problems. J. Soc. Ind. Appl. Math. **5**(1), 32–38 (1957)
9. Petroni, F., et al.: Language models as knowledge bases? In: Proceedings of the 2019 Conference on Empirical Methods in Natural Language Processing and the 9th International Joint Conference on Natural Language Processing (EMNLP-IJCNLP), pp. 2463–2473. Association for Computational Linguistics, Hong Kong, China (Nov 2019), https://aclanthology.org/D19-1250
10. Radford, A., Wu, J., Child, R., Luan, D., Amodei, D., Sutskever, I., et al.: Language models are unsupervised multitask learners. OpenAI Blog **1**(8), 9 (2019)
11. Raffel, C., et al.: Exploring the limits of transfer learning with a unified text-to-text transformer. J. Mach. Learn. Res. **21**(140), 1–67 (2020). http://jmlr.org/papers/v21/20-074.html
12. Sap, M., Rashkin, H., Chen, D., Le Bras, R., Choi, Y.: Social IQa: commonsense reasoning about social interactions. In: Proceedings of the 2019 Conference on Empirical Methods in Natural Language Processing and the 9th International Joint Conference on Natural Language Processing (EMNLP-IJCNLP). pp. 4463–4473. Association for Computational Linguistics, Hong Kong, China, November 2019. https://aclanthology.org/D19-1454
13. Shin, T., Razeghi, Y., Logan IV, R.L., Wallace, E., Singh, S.: AutoPrompt: eliciting knowledge from language models with automatically generated prompts. In: Proceedings of the 2020 Conference on Empirical Methods in Natural Language Processing (EMNLP), pp. 4222–4235. Association for Computational Linguistics, Online, November 2020. https://aclanthology.org/2020.emnlp-main.346
14. Talmor, A., Herzig, J., Lourie, N., Berant, J.: Commonsenseqa: a question answering challenge targeting commonsense knowledge. arXiv preprint arXiv:1811.00937 (2018)

A Scheduled Mask Method for TextVQA

Mingjie Han, Ting Jin(✉), and Wancong Lin

School of Computer Science and Technology, Hainan University,
Haikou 570228, China
jinting@hainanu.edu.cn

Abstract. At present, many successful applications use deep learning method in the field of Visual Question Answering (VQA). With the introduction of Optical Character Recognition (OCR), Text-based Visual Question Answering (TextVQA) tasks have a mature basic structure, a transformer-based iterative decoding prediction module. However, there is a problem in the current models: the training process of the model is inconsistent with the inference process. This inconsistency is shown in the different input and the different iteration prediction steps. We propose a scheduled mask method. After using this method, our model can gradually adapt to the situation without the ground truth answer input in the training process. We have verified the effectiveness of our method on the TextVQA dataset and exceeded the performance of other models previously proposed.

Keywords: Scheduled mask · TextVQA · Exposure bias

1 Introduction

Deep learning technology [1] has been developing rapidly recently. It has a good performance in the visual modality and language modality, such as object detection [2,3], semantic segmentation [4,5], image generation [6,7], text classification [8,9], information extraction [10,11], automatic summarization [12,13], etc. In recent years, some work has been done to process the information of visual modality and language modality using the same model to complete some complex tasks, such as classification and detection. In natural scenes, there are multiple inputs of text, pictures, and voice. When the human brain makes calculations and judgments, it sometimes does not rely solely on single-mode input, so multimodal information input is more consistent with natural scenes. The task of visual question answering simulates one of the scenes. Models calculate the answer according to the picture and the questions are given by the picture. When calculating, models need to read the content of the picture and the area related to the question, fuse and understand the multimodal features, and finally answer.

It is very common for a picture of a visual question answering task to contain text, for example, when the text is a shop sign, book title, and billboard slogan.

T. Yang et al. (Eds.): IOOO 9099, LNCS 13734, pp. 25–35, 2022.
https://doi.org/10.1007/978-3-031-23585-6_3

These characters are usually called OCR tokens and can be obtained by text detection and text recognition methods based on depth learning. With the help of these OCR tokens, the model can understand the relationship between objects and text in the picture scene, and can also help understand the content of objects through text. As shown in Fig. 1, according to the questions given, the model needs to locate the basketball first, then find the person holding the basketball, and finally find his number on the person's clothes. This is a progressive reasoning process. The model needs to model the relationship between basketball and players, and the relationship between players and numbers to answer questions. Without the participation of OCR text, the correct answer cannot be obtained.

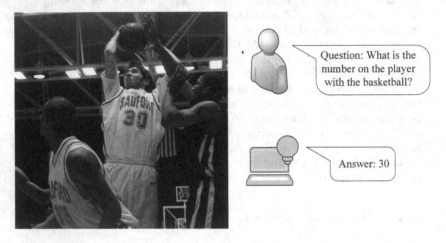

Fig. 1. An example of the TextVQA dataset. The model needs to predict a correct answer according to the given question.

In recent studies, most models have adopted an iterative decoding structure, using multi-step and multi-classification to complete the prediction of variable-length answers. For example, the M4C model [14] uses a multimodal Transformer structure to fuse features from questions, objects, OCR tokens, and answers. When multimodal features are fused, teacher-forcing is used. The answer features guide the fusion process. This mechanism can avoid the prediction error in the following steps caused by the prediction error in the previous step during training. In the sample of multi-word answers, the effect of this method is obvious. However, this method will also cause the following problem: the predicted scene is inconsistent with the training scene. The model will fit the given data during training, including the ground truth answers. If the model can achieve high accuracy in the training dataset, it shows that the model can correctly predict the results with the input of real answer data. However, the model did not learn how to predict without the ground truth answer input, which is exactly the inevitable scenario when predicting on the test dataset. The existing model cannot solve the inconsistency between training and prediction.

In this paper, we propose a scheduled mask method to solve the above problems. Gradually increasing the proportion of samples without the ground truth answers, help the model gradually adapt to the scenario without the ground truth answers. We propose three alternative mask change curves and verify their effectiveness on the M4C model [14].

Our contributions in this paper are summarized as follows: 1) We propose a scheduled mask strategy to reduce the difference between the training and inference steps. 2) Our scheduled mask method has good performance on the verification dataset and test dataset of TextVQA. It can reach the current state-of-the-art level.

2   Related Work

2.1   Text-Based Visual Question Answering

In 2019, Singh et al. [15] proposed the TextVQA dataset and LoRRA model, which added an OCR token copy module to the vocabulary to dynamically select answers. M4C [14] innovatively proposed an iterative decoding module, which uses autoregression to answer multi-word answers. SMA [16] regards the object and OCR text as nodes and the distance between the object and OCR text as edges to build a structure diagram. The decomposed problem features will update the corresponding different nodes and edges in the graph to generate global OCR marker features and visual object features. Based on SMA, TIG [17] cancels the connection between nodes that are too far away. The edge features in the structure graph will be updated constantly during training, which is more in line with the actual situation. The fusion method of problem features in a multimode attention fusion network is the fusion features of weighted transformer processing. In CRN [18], the progressive self-attention method is used for multimodal fusion. Progressive self-attention superimposes attention in the order of problem object OCR.

2.2   Teacher-Forcing and Exposure Bias

Teacher-forcing is a common method in recurrent neural networks (RNN) [19] to avoid errors being spread and learned in training. However, the inconsistency of input in training and inference leads to models cannot adapt to treat prediction as input for the next step. Bengio et al. [20] introduce the curriculum learning method in the decoding step to address the problem of different inputs. The Training process gradually changed from being guided by the ground truth tokens to being guided by the generated tokens. This way works well in image captioning, constituency parsing, and speech recognition. It is also used for reference by some subsequent methods and applied in other fields [21–23]. Ranzato et al. [24] propose to use model prediction at training time and introduce mixed incremental Cross-entropy reinforcement to optimize the final evaluation metric. Lamb et al. [25] introduce two adversarial channel structure shared parameters to force the model learning truth distribution. A discriminator is used to make the features guided by ground truth and prediction similar. Schmidt [26] rethinks this problem and proposes a simple regularization for better performance, which learns with reinforcement to extend maximum-likelihood.

The above research only deals with exposure bias in natural language processing. There is no method to deal with this problem in the multimodal TextVQA model at present. Therefore, we propose a scheduled mask method suitable for TextVQA tasks.

3   Method

Overview. In this paper, the prediction process of the common model is formulated in Sect. 3.2. And a Scheduled Mask Strategy is proposed to solve the inconsistency between the training step and the inference step to replace the previous decoder structure in Sect. 3.3.

3.1   Teacher-Forcing

Teacher-forcing is a mechanism that can avoid the wrong intermediate state affecting model learning, and is widely used in RNN and other networks. To be trained in the right direction, existing models usually use the ground truth answer words as the input information of the answer modality. Figure 2 shows the mask matrix of attention of a multi-modal transformer, as a fusion module. Questions, visual objects, OCR words, and answers are four modals of TextVQA task. Answers are attended to other modalities but other information will not influence answers. The ladder-shaped mask at the right bottom corner can ensure the correct word order of the predicted answers because the following word features will not affect the previous. However, teacher-forcing is not used in the inference step, which results in inconsistency of answer input.

3.2   Prediction Process

Given an image and a question, the whole prediction process is regarded as calculating the scores of each word in the variable vocabulary. The variable vocabulary is composed of fixed words, which includes S_{fix} words that appear most frequently on the training dataset and copying OCR tokens, which selects S_{cp} OCR tokens. As shown in Fig. 3, the difference between training and inference is that the model only predicts one time based on the ground truth answers in training and predicts T times based on a zero-vector in inference.

The process is further expressed by the formula. Given an input/output pair $\{X, Y\}$, the log probability is as

$$logP(Y|X) = logP(y_1^T|X) \tag{1}$$

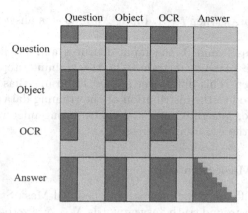

Fig. 2. The mask matrix of the self-attention in the multi-modal transformer. The gray parts of this matrix indicates features in these part cannot be involved in the calculation, but the orange part can. (Color figure online)

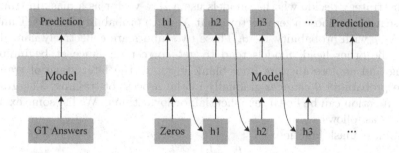

Fig. 3. Different prediction processes during training (left) and inference (right). Here are two differences: 1) Answer inputs. The ground truth answers are used to lead the training models while a zero-vector is fed into models in inference. 2) Prediction steps. Models only predict one time in training but predict T steps.

where T is the steps of prediction. Input X includes features of four different modalities while only the changes of answer features are considered here because other modalities are consistent. Then, the training process is formulated as

$$logP(y_1^T|X) = logP(y_1^T|X_{GT}) \tag{2}$$

where T is 1 in Eq. 2. Input X_{GT} indicates answer features are the ground truth. The prediction is depend entirely on the ground truth answers. The inference process is formulated as

$$logP(y_1^T|X) = logP(y_1^T|X_0)$$
$$= \sum_{t=1}^{T} logP(y^t|y^{t-1}) \tag{3}$$

where y^0 is equal to X_0 when $t = 1$. Input X_0 indicates answer features are one zero-vector.

As shown in Eqs. 2 and 3, the input features and prediction process are different. Thus, the parameters trained in the training step are not suitable for the inference step. This difference, named Exposure Bias, occurs when the model is only exposed to the distribution of the training dataset rather than its prediction. The error generated in $t = 0$ times during inference will propagate and accumulate as the iteration progresses.

3.3 Scheduled Mask Strategy

To eliminate this difference, we propose a Scheduled Mask Strategy. The input has two sources: the ground truth answer words X_{GT} or a zero-vector X_0. On the one head, a ground truth input speeds up convergence while models are unable to handle the zero-vector. Conversely, although a zero-vector makes the process of training and inference consistent, the performance is not good.

Our strategy decide whether models use a zero-vector as a mask in training. Suppose models choose a zero-vector input X_0 with probability θ, and GT answer input X_{GT} with probability $1 - \theta$. These two inputs are collectively named $\hat{X}$.

On the other head, models tend to get correct guidance at beginning of training and explore answers from blank input in the later stage of training. So, the probability θ changes gradually in the process of training. The gradual change function can be linear, exponential, or logarithmic. We list some example functions as follows:

1) Linear mask function:

$$\theta_i = k \cdot i + b \tag{4}$$

2) Exponential mask function:

$$\theta_i = \frac{k^i}{c} + b \tag{5}$$

3) Logarithmic mask function:

$$\theta_i = \log_k (i + b) \tag{6}$$

where θ_i is the mask probability. k provides the speed of change. c reduce the scope of change. b is the offset of function and it indicates the epoch starting masking. Then, an upper limit value and a lower limit value are added to the probability, and the final probability is as

$$\hat{\theta}_i = \min(\theta_{max}, \max(\theta_{min}, \theta_i)) \tag{7}$$

4 Experiments

The proposed scheduled sampling strategy is verified on M4C [14] model and in TextVQA [15] dataset.

4.1   Datasets and Evaluation Metrics

TextVQA is a text-based visual question answering dataset proposed by Singh in 2019 [15]. The images of this dataset come from the Open Image V3 dataset [27]. Question-and-answer pairs are derived from human annotation. Usually, there are one or two questions per picture, and each question is answered by ten people. In total, the dataset has 28,408 images, 45,336 questions, and 453,360 answers. The accuracy calculation index of each question adopts the soft score method based on the number of occurrences [28].

4.2   Experiment Settings and Training Details

The proposed scheduled sampling strategy is verified on M4C [14]. M4C provides a basic solution framework for the TextVQA task, and many subsequent studies and models are based on this work. Therefore, the verification work on this model also has reference significance for other subsequent models.

The visual features of the target are extracted by Faster R-CNN. To ensure accuracy, Faster R-CNN is pretrained on the Visual Genome dataset. The Visual Genome dataset is a large-scale image semantic understanding dataset. Each image contains a question-answer pair. This dataset can help the model understand the relationship between objects in natural scenes without annotation. OCR words are extracted by the Rosetta system. This is a deployable and scalable OCR system proposed by Facebook in 2019. The system can easily get OCR text information and location information. The semantic features of the question are extracted with Bert. Bert is a large-scale language pretraining model. In 2018, it broke multiple records in the field of natural language processing. The multimodal Transformer structure is used for feature fusion, using the latest self-attention mechanism to fully fuse multimodal features. A dynamic pointer network is used to classify and select the words to answer the question, which ensures that each sample is answered based on the OCR text on its image.

We use a batch size of 128 and train our model for 24000 iterations. We use the Adam optimizer with an initial learning rate of 0.0001, multiplied by 0.1 at 14000 and 19000 iterations. Also, the warmup schedule is used for the first 1000 iterations with a factor of 0.2. Training and inference take about 7 h with one NVIDIA 3090 GPU.

4.3   Comparison with State-of-the-Art

TextVQA Dataset. The superiority of our scheduled mask method in improving model accuracy is shown in Table 1. Line 1 is the state-of-the-art model of the TextVQA task, line 2 to line 6 are the improved models based on M4C [14], and the line 7 M4C+SM (M4C with scheduled mask) is the result of our scheduled mask method based on M4C. To make the comparison more fairer, all models use the Rosetta-en [29] system to extract OCR tokens, and all models do not use extra visual question answering data. Our method improves M4C by 1.56%, outperforming the BOV [30] model by about 0.06%.

We use the logarithmic mask curve in the data in line 7 because it is validated as the best-performing curve, which is discussed in Sect. 4.4.

However, the effect of our model on the test dataset is not obvious in line 8. This shows that the generalization ability of our model on unknown datasets needs to be improved. We find that the mask process has a startup problem. In the process of input data being masked gradually, some data is ignored firstly, and the other remaining data determines the generalization ability of the model on the unknown dataset. On the TextVQA dataset [15], the best model which fits the startup data on the verification set cannot be adapted to the test dataset.

Table 1. Results of different state-of-the-art models on TextVQA dataset.

Model	Val acc. (%)	Test acc. (%)
M4C [14]	39.40	39.01
SMA [16]	40.05	40.66
SSBaseline [31]	40.38	40.92
CRN [18]	40.39	40.96
TIG [17]	40.45	–
LAaP-Net [32]	40.68	40.54
BOV [30]	40.90	**41.23**
M4C+SM (Ours)	**40.96**	40.70

4.4   Ablation Study

We augmented with different mask curves on the M4C model, as shown in Table 2. All the results show that our method enables the model to learn not only the features of the ground truth answer input but also learn the computation method with a zero vector input. The improved model can test directly after training. Lines 2 to 4 illustrate the final results of different curves. It can be seen that the effect of logarithmic and exponential curves is similar, and the effect of logarithmic curve is slightly better than that of the exponential curve. Both curves work better than linear curves. This shows that more complex curves can bring better results.

Table 2. Results of ablation experiments of our model on TextVQA dataset.

Models	Mask functions	Val acc. (%)
M4C [14]	–	39.40
M4C+SM	linear	40.66
M4C+SM	exponential	40.92
M4C+SM	logarithmic	**40.96**

In addition, we also compared the accuracy and prediction per second (PPS) of the M4C model and the M4C+SM model at different prediction iteration steps, as shown in Table 3. With the scheduled mask, the accuracy of M4C+SM model is always better than M4C at different iteration steps. And the performance of M4C+SM in iteration step 3 is equal to that of M4C in iteration step 12. This shows the superiority of our scheduled mask.

Table 3. The FPS and accuracy in different iteration steps on the M4C model and the M4C+SM model.

Models	Iteration steps	PPS	Val acc. (%)
M4C [14]	12	7.12	39.40
M4C [14]	9	9.92	39.25
M4C [14]	6	12.48	39.01
M4C [14]	3	15.15	38.82
M4C+SM	12	7.45	40.96
M4C+SM	9	9.92	40.12
M4C+SM	6	12.67	39.47
M4C+SM	3	14.96	39.42

5   Conclusion

A scheduled mask method is proposed to solve the exposure bias problem in the TextVQA model. With the training process, the input of the model gradually changes from the ground truth answer input to the no answer input. This change allows the model to adapt to the testing process. Among the three proposed scheduled curves, the logarithmic curve is verified to be the best. The performance of M4C+SM on the TextVQA dataset exceeds that of other models previously proposed. However, the problem of decreasing the accuracy caused by reducing the number of iteration steps has not been solved. And our scheduled mask method has a startup problem. In future work, we will continue to study and improve these problems.

Acknowledgment. This work was supported by National Science Foundation of China (No. 61862021) and Hainan Provincial Natural Science Foundation of China (No. 620RC565).

References

1. LeCun, Y., Bengio, Y., Hinton, G.: Deep learning. Nature **521**(7553), 436–444 (2015)
2. Zhao, Z.Q., Zheng, P., Xu, S.t., Wu, X.: Object detection with deep learning: a review. IEEE Trans. Neural Networks Learn. Syst. **30**(11), 3212–3232 (2019)

3. Amit, Y., Felzenszwalb, P., Girshick, R.: Object detection. Computer Vision : A Reference Guide, pp. 1–9 (2020)
4. Wang, P., Chen, P., Yuan, Y., Liu, D., Huang, Z., Hou, X., Cottrell, G.: Understanding convolution for semantic segmentation. In: 2018 IEEE Winter Conference on Applications of Computer Vision (WACV), pp. 1451–1460. IEEE (2018)
5. Guo, Y., Liu, Y., Georgiou, T., Lew, M.S.: A review of semantic segmentation using deep neural networks. Int. J. Multimed. Inf. Retrieval 7(2), 87–93 (2018)
6. Gregor, K., Danihelka, I., Graves, A., Rezende, D., Wierstra, D.: Draw: a recurrent neural network for image generation. In: International Conference on Machine Learning, PMLR, pp. 1462–1471 (2015)
7. Qiao, T., Zhang, J., Xu, D., Tao, D.: Mirrorgan: learning text-to-image generation by redescription. In: Proceedings of the IEEE/CVF Conference on Computer Vision and Pattern Recognition, pp. 1505–1514 (2019)
8. Kowsari, K., Jafari Meimandi, K., Heidarysafa, M., Mendu, S., Barnes, L., Brown, D.: Text classification algorithms: a survey. Information 10(4), 150 (2019)
9. Mirończuk, M.M., Protasiewicz, J.: A recent overview of the state-of-the-art elements of text classification. Expert Syst. Appl. 106, 36–54 (2018)
10. Piskorski, J., Yangarber, R.: Information extraction: past, present and future. In: Multi-source, Multilingual Information Extraction and Summarization, pp. 23–49. Springer (2013)
11. Olivetti, E.A., Cole, J.M., Kim, E., Kononova, O., Ceder, G., Han, T.Y.J., Hiszpanski, A.M.: Data-driven materials research enabled by natural language processing and information extraction. Appl. Phys. Rev. 7(4), 041317 (2020)
12. Haque, S., LeClair, A., Wu, L., McMillan, C.: Improved automatic summarization of subroutines via attention to file context. In: Proceedings of the 17th International Conference on Mining Software Repositories, pp. 300–310 (2020)
13. Moreno, L., Marcus, A.: Automatic software summarization: the state of the art. In: Proceedings of the 40th International Conference on Software Engineering: Companion Proceeedings, pp. 530–531 (2018)
14. Hu, R., Singh, A., Darrell, T., Rohrbach, M.: Iterative answer prediction with pointer-augmented multimodal transformers for textvqa. In: Proceedings of the IEEE/CVF Conference on Computer Vision and Pattern Recognition, pp. 9992–10002 (2020)
15. Singh, A., et al.: Towards vqa models that can read. In: Proceedings of the IEEE/CVF Conference on Computer Vision and Pattern Recognition, pp. 8317–8326 (2019)
16. Gao, C., et al.: Structured multimodal attentions for textvqa. IEEE Trans. Pattern Anal. Mach. Intell. (2021)
17. Li, X., Wu, B., Song, J., Gao, L., Zeng, P., Gan, C.: Text-instance graph: exploring the relational semantics for text-based visual question answering. Pattern Recogn. 124, 108455 (2022)
18. Liu, F., Xu, G., Wu, Q., Du, Q., Jia, W., Tan, M.: Cascade reasoning network for text-based visual question answering. In: Proceedings of the 28th ACM International Conference on Multimedia, pp. 4060–4069 (2020)
19. Mikolov, T., Karafiát, M., Burget, L., Cernocký, J., Khudanpur, S.: Recurrent neural network based language model. In: Interspeech. Volume 2, Makuhari, pp. 1045–1048 (2010)
20. Bengio, S., Vinyals, O., Jaitly, N., Shazeer, N.: Scheduled sampling for sequence prediction with recurrent neural networks. In: Advances in Neural Information Processing Systems 28 (2015)

21. Yu, L., Zhang, W., Wang, J., Yu, Y.: Seqgan: sequence generative adversarial nets with policy gradient. In: Proceedings of the AAAI Conference on Artificial Intelligence, vol. 31 (2017)
22. Finn, C., Goodfellow, I., Levine, S.: Unsupervised learning for physical interaction through video prediction. In: Advances in Neural Information Processing Systems 29 (2016)
23. Martinez, J., Black, M.J., Romero, J.: On human motion prediction using recurrent neural networks. In: Proceedings of the IEEE Conference on Computer Vision and Pattern Recognition, pp. 2891–2900 (2017)
24. Ranzato, M., Chopra, S., Auli, M., Zaremba, W.: Sequence level training with recurrent neural networks. arXiv preprint arXiv:1511.06732 (2015)
25. Lamb, A.M., Alias Parth Goyal, A.G., Zhang, Y., Zhang, S., Courville, A.C., Bengio, Y.: Professor forcing: A new algorithm for training recurrent networks. Advances in neural information processing systems 29 (2016)
26. Schmidt, F.: Generalization in generation: A closer look at exposure bias. arXiv preprint arXiv:1910.00292 (2019)
27. Krasin, I., et al.: Openimages: a public dataset for large-scale multi-label and multi-class image classification. Dataset available from https://github.com/openimages 2(3) (2017) 18
28. Antol, S., Agrawal, A., Lu, J., Mitchell, M., Batra, D., Zitnick, C.L., Parikh, D.: Vqa: visual question answering. In: Proceedings of the IEEE International Conference on Computer Vision, pp. 2425–2433 (2015)
29. Borisyuk, F., Gordo, A., Sivakumar, V.: Rosetta: large scale system for text detection and recognition in images. In: Proceedings of the 24th ACM SIGKDD International Conference on Knowledge Discovery & Data Mining, pp. 71–79 (2018)
30. Zeng, G., Zhang, Y., Zhou, Y., Yang, X.: Beyond ocr+ vqa: involving ocr into the flow for robust and accurate textvqa. In: Proceedings of the 29th ACM International Conference on Multimedia (2021) 376–385
31. Zhu, Q., Gao, C., Wang, P., Wu, Q.: Simple is not easy: A simple strong baseline for textvqa and textcaps. arXiv preprint arXiv:2012.05153 2 (2020)
32. Han, W., Huang, H., Han, T.: Finding the evidence: Localization-aware answer prediction for text visual question answering. arXiv preprint arXiv:2010.02582 (2020)

Application Track

A Coarse-to-Fine Text Matching Framework for Customer Service Question Answering

Ang Li[1,3], Xingwei Liang[2], Miao Zhang[2], Bingbing Wang[1,3], Guanrong Chen[1,3], Jun Gao[1,3], Qihui Lin[1,3], and Ruifeng Xu[1,3(✉)]

[1] School of Computer Science and Technology, Harbin Institute of Technology (Shenzhen), Shenzhen, China
{22s151165,22s151179,1171000607,190110527}@stu.hit.edu.cn
[2] Konka Corporation, Shenzhen, China
{liangxingwei,zhangmiao3}@konka.com
[3] Joint Lab of HIT and KONKA, Shenzhen, China
xuruifeng@hit.edu.cn

Abstract. Customer service question answering have recently seen increased interest in NLP due to their potential commercial values. However, existing methods are largely based on Deep Neural Networks (DNNs) that are computationally expensive and memory intensive, which hinder their deployment in many real-world scenarios. In addition, the customer service dialogue data is very domain-specific, and it is difficult to achieve a high matching accuracy without specific model optimization. In this paper, we propose **CFTM**, A **C**oarse-to-**F**ine **T**ext **M**atching Framework, which consists of Fasttext coarse-grained classification, and Roformer-sim fine-grained sentence vector matching. This Coarse-to-Fine structure can effectively reduce the amount of model parameters and speed up system inference. We also use the CoSENT loss function to optimize the Roformer-sim model according to the characteristics of customer service dialogue data, which effectively improves the matching accuracy of the framework. We conduct extensive experiments on CHUZHOU and EIP customer service questioning datasets from KONKA. The result shows that CFTM outperforms baselines across all metrics, achieving a 2.5 improvement in F1-Score and a 30% improvement in inference time, which demonstrates that our CFTM gets higher response accuracy and faster interaction speed in customer service question answering.

Keywords: Customer service question answering · Natural language processing · Text matching · Deep neural network

1 Introduction

In different application scenarios, the Natural Language Processing (NLP) tasks challenged by customer service question answering covers a wide range. Most

---

A. Li and X. Liang—These authors contributed equally to this work.

ⓒ The Author(s), under exclusive license to Springer Nature Switzerland AG 2022
Y. Yang et al. (Eds.): ICCC 2022, LNCS 13734, pp. 00–50, 2022.
https://doi.org/10.1007/978-3-031-23585-6_4

existing question answering systems focus on Spoken Language Understanding (SLU) and Natural Language Generation (NLG), which provides cross-domain chatting capabilities [1]. However, in customer service question answering system, we often need to preset specific answers based on specific types of questions (such as solving customer's after-sales problems) Therefore, in current customer service question answering methods, text matching models are often used to classify user questions and return specific answers [2].

Traditional text matching most depended on manual feature searching methods like TF-IDF and BM25. With the emergency and unceasing development of deep learning, text sequence matching can be summarized into two types consisting of interaction based matching and representation based matching. The interaction based matching method splices the query and the sentences for binary classification, which can better integrate the features between the query and the sentences, so the matching accuracy is higher. While the representation based matching method calculates the sentence vector of the query and the sentences, and then performs vector similarity matching, which has the advantages of faster matching speed and higher extensibility.

DSSM, a representation based matching method proposed by Microsoft [3] opens the door of deep learning technology in text matching task. DSSM model embeds and encodes the two pieces of text that need to be matched, obtains their semantic vector representation through multi-layer perceptron, and finally obtains the similarity of the text through cosine similarity, which establishes the basic paradigm of representation based matching. Microsoft continued to put forward CDSSM [4] in the next year, of which MLP was replaced with a more advanced Convolutional Neural Network (CNN). Similarly, the deep convolution structure ARC I [5] derived by Huawei for matching natural language sentences emerged as the times require. Otherwise, Mueller et al. [6] proposed an LSTM based Siamese network model for marker data composed of variable length sequence pairs, which is superior to well-designed features and more complex neural network systems. However, the innovation of the representation based matching method is limited since its key is how to better obtain the representation vector of a single text. In the work of Wan et al. [7], the main disadvantage of representation based matching model that important local information would be lost when such a complex sentence is compressed into a single vector, is pointed out Therefore, interaction based text sequence matching model arises at the historic moment.

Under the interaction based matching methods, the smaller units of two sentences such as words or context vectors are first matched, and then the matching results are aggregated into vectors to obtain the final result [2]. For example, on the basis of ARC I, Hu et al. proposed the architecture ARC II [5] directly relied on the interaction space between two sentences to obtain the n-gram level representation of two sentences through one layer of CNN. Furthermore, MV-LSTM [7] applies Bi-LSTM to enhancing encoding of embedding, so as to complement ARC II. Meanwhile, Match-Pyramid [8] proposes a variety of matching modes when calculating the interaction matrix. Gradually, attention mechanism has become a core of text matching since it can capture global connections. BiMPM [9] summarized the mode of attention mechanism and described the paradigm of interaction based matching model. Cross attention is adopted in ESIM [10] to calculate the final characterization vector, which has become a common method in subsequent research. In recent years, the pre-training model has shown amazing performance in NLP tasks, including text matching. Qiao et al. [11]. found that comparing the effects of several different fusion strategies based on Bert [12], the results showed that it was better to use [CLS] output vector classification directly than to interact or aggregate the vectors output by Bert.

Since the interaction based matching method needs to continuously combine sentence pairs for reasoning, the retrieval efficiency is far less than that of the representation based method. Reimers et al. hence proposed Sentence-Bert [13] using concatenation and triple network structure to deduce semantically meaningful text sentence embedding, thus greatly speeding up the reasoning. In addition, for interaction based models, similar behaviors of expanding and migrating knowledge base often mean that the model needs to be retrained and have a great impact on final performance. However, the representation based model can theoretically transform new knowledge sentences into good semantic embedding even without training. The RoFormer-Sim [14] proposed by Su et al. can also better obtain sentence vectors and achieve retrieval objectives.

Based on the current problems and the above research, in this paper, we present **CFTM**, A **C**oarse-to-**F**ine **T**ext **M**atching Framework. In this framework, we first use the Fasttext network for coarse-grained classification, and directly output the results with high classification confidence as matching results. For samples with low classification confidence, we input them into the fine-grained text matching network in the latter layer, use the Roformer-sim model which optimized by the CoSENT loss function to encode the sentence vector, and use Faiss for vector calculation to obtain fine-grained match result. The experimental section below shows that our CFTM outperforms the baseline model in matching accuracy, model inference time, and interception rate, demonstrating the effectiveness of CFTM. The main contributions of this paper are illustrated as follows:

(1) Using the Coarse-to-Fine text matching framework. First use the shallow network Fasttext to classify the user query, and when the confidence is lower than the threshold, then input the sample to the Roformer-sim network. This process greatly speeds up the average inference speed of the overall structure of the CFTM and shortens the response delay of the system.

(2) Using the sentence vector encoding based on the Roformer-sim model, compared with the interactive text matching model, it has faster coding and matching speed.

(3) The modified CoSENT loss function is used to optimize the Roformer-sim model, which improves the model matching accuracy and model convergence speed.

The remaining part of this paper is organized as follows. Section 2 presents the application background that this paper focuses on and problem definition.

Section 3 introduces our proposed framework in detail, and next in Sect. 4 we introduce our experiments and present results for analysis. Section 5 summarizes the entire work.

2 Preliminary

In this section, we introduce the application background that this paper mainly focuses on and the related problem definition.

2.1 Application Background

At present, most customer service question answering system often use cloud computing. The model calculation that consumes a lot of computing power is completed in the cloud, and the edge server is only responsible for simple data processing and interaction. Such deployment method is extremely dependent on the connection quality of the network. In the case of no network connection or poor connection quality, the cloud computing-based customer service question answering system will not work properly. Therefore, this paper mainly discusses the possibility and optimization method of deploying a complete customer service question answering system on the edge server. Usually, the computing resources of the edge server are very limited. If the offline model is directly deployed to the edge, the parameters and computational complexity of the model need to be limited. In this paper, we limit the amount of model parameters and computational complexity, and optimizes the matching accuracy, and interaction time of the customer service question answering system.

2.2 Problem Definition

Common solutions of customer service question answering are mainly based on two different methods. The most common method is based on text sequence matching. By comparing the matching degree between the standard questions in the knowledge base and the user's questions, it is a direct and efficient method to answer the user's questions with the standard output. The other is based on the method of generating answers using a deep neural network model, which needs to apply the results of related NLP tasks such as Spoken Language Understanding (SLU) and Natural Language Generation (NLG). The method of generating answers based on models is often prone to logical and semantic incorrect results, and requires complex components to combine into a comparatively perfect model, which is not mature at present. This paper mainly discusses the method based on text sequence matching. According to similar existing literature [15,16], text sequence matching can be defined as: given two texts $Text_1$ and $Text_2$, their matching degree is usually modeled as the score generated by the scoring function based on the representation of each text:

$$match\left(Text_1, Text_2\right) = F\left(\Phi\left(Text_1\right), \Phi\left(Text_2\right)\right) \tag{1}$$

where Φ is a function that converts the text into a representation vector, and F is a function that performs matching scoring based on the interactions between two representation vectors. According to how to select Φ and F, text sequence matching can be categorized into three types: keyword based method, representation based method and interaction based method. The deep matching models mainly uses the latter two methods. The method based on keyword matching actually does not convert the two texts into a representation vector, but manually constructs a feature function that can represent the matching degree based on the words in the two sentences:

$$match\left(Text_1, Text_2\right) = F\left(Text_1, Text_2\right). \tag{2}$$

The performance of the results depends on the design of features, so the generalization ability is often not as good as the deep learning model. And because of the limitation of the number of manually selected features, the model can't be designed like the depth neural network, and its performance is often easy to reach the bottleneck.

The key of the text sequence matching model based on representation is to get an excellent representation vector of a single text. Then a function is designed to match the two texts in such a vector space. Therefore, Φ of this method is a complex mapping function while F is a relatively simple matching function. For example, Φ in DSSM [3] is a feed forward neural network, and F is a cosine similarity function. In C-DSSM [4], Φ is changed to a convolutional neural network. In ARC-I [5], F is changed to a multi-layer perceptron. In sentence-BERT [13], Φ is changed to a frame dominated by BERT [12]. The model under this framework will not affect each other when each text is mapped into a representation vector. For example, when applied to customer service question answering, the representation vector of the standard question in the knowledge base can be saved in advance to accelerate reasoning. In addition, it often has a good migration ability to different databases because Φ has a good mapping to a single text. But its disadvantage is also obvious, that is, it ignores the matching of local features in sentence pairs and thus the accuracy is often not as excellent as the matching model based on interaction.

The text sequence matching model based on interaction is more complex. It first interacts with the basic representations of the two texts locally, and then uses neural networks to learn hierarchical interaction patterns for matching. Therefore, contrary to the representation model, Φ here is often a simple mapping function, while F is a complex deep neural network model. For example, Φ in ARC-II [5] is a sentence embedding mapped by a basic unsupervised word embedding method, and F is a convolutional neural network on two text interaction matrices. After that, the extensive application of the attention mechanism made every model make great efforts in text interaction. This framework mines the local feature interaction in sentence pairs, and its accuracy is higher than that of the representation based model. Since the improvement space of this method is often designed at the level of sentence pair interaction, there are many innovations. But inevitably, the retrieval efficiency of this method is much

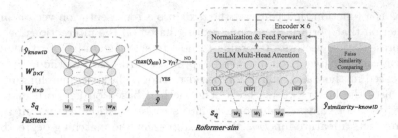

Fig. 1. CFTM Coarse-to-Fine text matching framework.

slower than that of the representation based method, and its portability is not as good as that of the representation based model.

3 Methodology

3.1 Coarse-to-Fine Framework

Coarse-to-Fine Framework shown in Fig. 1 is adopted in CFTM for text matching. Given user query s_q after the unified tokenizer, query is first input to Fasttext [17], a shallow neural network for preliminary classification to obtain the result $\hat{y}_q$. When $max(\hat{y}_q)$ is greater than the threshold γ_{ft}, the matching result $argmax(\hat{y}_q)$ with the highest confidence will be output as the final result. On the contrary, s_q would be input to the followed Roformer-sim network to attain sentence embedding e_q. The cosine similarity between e_q and the sentence embedding $\{e_1, e_2, e_3, ..., e_N\}$ in knowledge base is calculated to get the similarity score $S \in \mathbb{R}^{N \times 1}$. On the one hand, $argmax(S)$ with highest similarity would be output if $max(S)$ is better than the similarity threshold ϕ_0. Otherwise, the corresponding standard question greater than the similarity threshold ϕ_1 in S is given as a guide question to guide the user to continue asking questions. The threshold γ_{ft}, ϕ_0 and ϕ_1 hyper-parameters described in Sect. 4.7 for details.

3.2 FastText

Fasttext [17] shown in the Fig. 1 is a fast text classification algorithm, which can accelerate the training and reasoning speed while maintaining high classification accuracy compared with the classification algorithm based on neural network.

Given an original sample of s, its real knowledge category is y. Fasttext uses the n-gram features $\{x_1, x_2, ..., x_N\}$of all words in the sample s as input:

$$h = \frac{1}{N} \sum_{i=1}^{N} W_{ih}^T x_i \tag{3}$$

$$\hat{y} = softmax(W_{ho}^T sigmoid(h)) \tag{4}$$

W_{IH}^t represents the weight input to the hidden layer, W_{ho}^T represents the weight from the hidden layer to the output layer, and $\hat{y}$ is the classification result output by the model. Besides, for the case where the classification category K is small, the multi classification cross entropy loss can be directly used as bellow:

$$J_{CE} = -\sum_{i=1}^{N}\sum_{k=1}^{K} y_i^k \log\left(\hat{y}_i^k\right) = -\sum_{i=1}^{N} y_i^{c_i} \log\left(\hat{y}_i^{c_i}\right) \tag{5}$$

When the number of target classifications K is large, if the standard softmax goes on line, K values need to be normalized and will occupy a large amount of calculation time. CFTM hence uses Fasttext with hierarchical softmax to construct Huffman tree according to the frequency of categories to replace the flattened standard softmax and improve the training speed. Huffman tree is a binary classification tree, and each leaf node in the tree represents a label. For each parent node, the sigmoid function is used to classify it, and finally the probability classification $\hat{y}$ of each leaf node is obtained.

3.3 Roformer-sim

Roformer-sim based on the Rofomer model integrates the attention mechanism of UniLM, and adopts comparative learning to conduct unsupervised pre-training tasks including generation task and classification task. Given s_A and s_B is a group of similar sentence pairs.

$[CLS]$ s_a $[SEP]$ s_b $[SEP]$ and $[CLS]$ s_b $[SEP]$ s_a $[SEP]$ are the input to Roformer-sim for the generation task with pre-training. At the same time, Roformer-sim takes the encoded vector of $[CLS]$ position as the sentence vector of the whole text. And the vector l_2 of $[CLS]$ in the whole batch after normalization, get the matrix of sentence vector $E \in \mathbb{R}^{b \times d}$ as well as the similarity matrix $S = EE^{\mathsf{T}} \in \mathbb{R}^{d \times d}$. Roformer-sim regards all similar samples as positive samples and non similar samples as negative samples for pre-training as classification tasks. Therefore, after unsupervised pre-training of a large number of similar sentences on the corpus, Roformer-sim has a strong ability to encode sentence vectors.

Faiss is shown in Fig. 2, an open source library of python which provides an efficient and reliable retrieval method for massive data in high-dimensional space, is applied to speed up the vector calculation and optimize the vector retrieval process.

We first use Roformer-sim to encode the text $\{s_1, s_2, ..., s_n\}$ in the knowledge base into a sentence vector matrix $e \in \mathbb{R}^{n \times d}$, where each sentence vector is d dimension. Then, Faiss creates an index data structure ($Index_E$) in memory.

When entering sentence vector e_q of user query s_q, e_q with the top k sentence vectors with the highest cosine similarity of and the corresponding cosine similarity can be efficiently returned by $Index_E$, so as to speed up vector retrieval, optimize the storage of vectors. After external knowledge encoded by Roformer-sim can be added to the index structure $Index_E$ to expand the knowledge base without retraining the model.

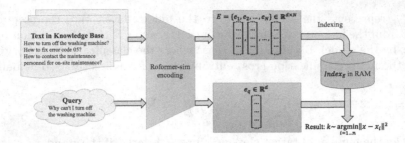

Fig. 2. Encode sentence vectors through roformer and use faiss for vector retrieval.

3.4   Model Optimization

Although Roformer-sim uses a large number of similar pairs of corpora for pre-training, it still uses the semi-supervised training method of similar sentences to the corpus in essence, which is still far from the knowledge base text used by customer service question answering. The traditional supervised fine-tuning of text matching uses a loss function based on $cos(U, V)$, for example, given a positive sample pair (x_{org}, x_{pos}) and a negative sample pair (x_{org}, x_{neg}):

$$loss = t \times (1 - \cos(x_{org}, x_{pos})) + (1 - t) \times (1 + \cos(x_{org}, x_{neg})) \quad (6)$$

$$loss = t \times (1 - \cos(x_{org}, x_{pos}))^2 + (1 - t) \times (1 + \cos(x_{org}, x_{neg}))^2 \quad (7)$$

The loss function considers that the target of the positive sample pair is 1, and the negative one is −1. However, the negative sample pairs are mostly samples with different semantics in the actual application scenario of customer service question answering, and there are many overlapping words. Take the text of the knowledge base inside KONKA as an example, as shown in the Table 1.

If directly use the formula (6) to optimize the negative samples with high text coincidence directly at −1, it will lead to over learning and poor optimization effect. However, inspired by CoSENT [18], which believes the similarity between positive sample pairs is still greater than that of negative sample pairs. In this paper, We made modifications to the way CoSENT constructs positive and negative sample pairs, and proposed a method of supervised fine tuning of Roformer-sim model on specific knowledge base data. We divides the knowledge base text into three tuples {original sample, similar sample, and non similar sample}. The similar sample is the sample with the same knowledge as the original sample, and the non similar sample is the sample with different knowledge from the original sample. Three tuples are encoded into sentence vectors by Roformer-sim to obtain $(e_{org}, e_{sim}, e_{unsim})$. After that, the loss function of supervised fine-tuning is set as the distance between the cosine similarity between the original sample and the similar sample and the cosine similarity between the original sample and the non similar sample, that is:

$$loss = \log(1 + \sum e^{\lambda(cos(e_{org}, e_{sim}) - cos(e_{org}, e_{unsim}))}) \quad (8)$$

Table 1. Negative sample pair examples in CHUZHOU knowledge base. In the same cell are negative sample pairs composed of different knowledge IDs. Italic words in "()" are the English translation of the original Chinese texts on their left.

Knowledge No.1045: 电视机出现线条怎么办?	*(What should I do if there are lines on the TV?)*
Knowledge No.1044: 电视机出现屏闪烁怎么办?	*(What should I do if the TV screen flickers?)*
Knowledge No.1096: 如何查询电视机的分辨率?	*(How to check the resolution of a TV?)*
Knowledge No.1099: 如何调节液晶电视分辨率?	*(How to adjust LCD TV resolution?)*
Knowledge No.1051: 电视机声音异常怎么办?	*(What should I do if the sound of the TV is abnormal?)*
Knowledge No.1048: 电视图像异常怎么办?	*(What should I do if the TV image is abnormal?)*

Table 2. Detailed statistics of CHUZHOU and EIP datasets. "#Knowledge" means the number of all knowledge, "#Sen" means the number of all sentences, "Avg. #Sims" signifies the average number of similar questions per knowledge.

Dataset	Topic	#Knowledge	#Sen	Avg. #Sims	Train	test
CHUZHOU	hardware troubleshoot	493	11010	22	8741	2269
EIP	business enquiry	153	2291	15	1827	464

λ is a hyper-parameter. This loss function can effectively avoid the problem of over optimization of the loss function based on $cos(U, V)$, effectively improve the speed and accuracy of model convergence, and improve the accuracy of text matching.

4 Experiment

This section mainly introduces the datasets, baseline models, experimental setup, and experimental results.

4.1 Datasets

We use the knowledge base datasets **CHUZHOU** and **EIP** from Konka Company to conduct experiments. These two datasets contain data columns: the serial number corresponding to each knowledge, the standard question corresponding to the knowledge, and the multiple similar questions corresponding to the knowledge. In this paper, multiple similar questions of each knowledge are divided into training set and test set according to the ratio of 7:3, which are used for fine-tuning and testing on downstream tasks. The specific datasets description is shown in Table 2.

4.2 Baselines

Usually, local edge servers require the parameter amount of the model to be less than 20M. Therefore, we choose two lightweight SOTA models based on knowledge distillation methods proposed in recent years: $TinyBert_4$ Chinese (the total number of parameters is 11.46M) and Ernie-3.0-nano-zh (the total number of parameters is 17.91M) as the baseline models. TinyBert [19] proposes a novel transformer distillation method, which introduces a two-stage distillation framework. When the model performance is similar to Bert, the model size is less than 1/7 of it, and the inference speed is more than 9 times. Ernie-3.0 [20] designs a unified pre-training framework that integrates auto-encoding networks and auto-regressive networks, and pre-trained on a 4TB corpus including plain text and knowledge graphs, outperforming the state-of-the-art on various NLP tasks. Ernie-3.0-nano is a lightweight model based on Ernie-3.0 and obtained through online distillation technology. Compared with the model with the same amount of parameters, it also achieves the SOTA effect on the CLUE task. In this paper, we use the pre-training parameters of $TinyBert_4$ Chinese and Ernie-3.0-nano-zh published on hugging face. For these two models, we use two text matching methods, interactive model(**IM**) and feature model(**FM**), also use the same dataset for fine-tuning and testing, and compare with the CFTM framework proposed in this paper.

4.3 Experimental Settings

For CFTM, we train the two parts of the Coarse-to-Fine text matching framework separately, and load the trained model parameters for testing. For fasttest, Word N Gram is set to 1, dimension is set to 340, epoch is set to 20, lr is set to 0.5. For Roformer-sim, we choose the small version with the parameter size of 15.35M, and load the pre-training parameters from the hugging face. For the baselines, we retain their recommended experimental settings. For all models in CFTM and baseline, we use onnx for deployment and model inference. onnx (Open Neural Network Exchange) is an open format for representing deep learning models proposed by Microsoft and Facebook. It defines a set of standard formats that are independent of the environment and platform, and is optimized for the inference speed of the model. All experiments in this paper are carried out on Intel Xeon Gold 5218R CPU and Tesla V100 GPU environment, and only CPU is used during testing.

4.4 Evaluation Metrics

To comprehensively consider the performance and interaction efficiency of the customer service question answering methods, we select the matching accuracy and model inference time as the evaluation metrics. The matching accuracy is defined as the proportion of samples that are correctly classified by Fasttext or correctly matched by Roformer-sim, and in this paper, we use weighted F1-Score to evaluate matching accuracy. The model inference time is defined as

Table 3. F1-Score and model inference time of CFTM and baseline models. Where "IM" means the interactive model, "FM" means the feature model, "(11.46 M)" means that the amount of model parameters is 11.46 million.

Model	CHUZHOU		EIP	
	F1-Score	infer time (ms)	F1-Score	infer time (ms)
TinyBert$_4$ Chinese IM (11.46M)	0.7405	42.4	0.8545	34.6
TinyBert$_4$ Chinese FM (11.46M)	0.7429	9.1	0.8512	7.9
Ernie-3.0-nano-zh IM (17.91M)	0.7596	41.9	0.8340	35.7
Ernie-3.0-nano-zh FM (17.91M)	0.7389	9.0	0.8590	8.2
CFTM (15.35M)	**0.7840**	**6.6**	**0.8890**	**6.9**

the average time for each sample to obtain the matching result through model inference. In addition, we show the change of the interception rate and accuracy rate of the customer service question answering methods with the change of the threshold ϕ_0. The interception rate here is defined as the proportion of samples whose matching result confidence is greater than the interception threshold ϕ_0, that is, the proportion of samples that the system believe can be responded effectively. The accuracy rate is defined as the proportion of correct matches in the intercepted samples, which is also evaluated using F1-Score.

4.5 Performance

First, we fix ϕ_0 to 0 to get all predictions from models. We compared our CFTM and all baseline models on the CHUZHOU and EIP datasets, the results are shown in the Fig. 3. We highlight in bold the highest F1-Score and shortest inference time. From this Table, We can observe that CFTM outperforms baselines across all metrics, achieving a 2.5 improvement in F1-Score and a 30% improvement in inference time. This demonstrates that our CFTM gets higher response accuracy and faster interaction speed in customer service question answering.

Table 3 shows the interception rate and F1-Score of CFTM and all baselines when the threshold ϕ_0 changes. We can indicate that under the same interception rate(column perspective), our CFTM has a higher F1-Score than baseline models, and under the same F1-Score(row perspective),our CFTM has a higher interception rate and can correctly handle more hard-to-classify samples.

4.6 Ablation Analysis

In this part, we disassemble CFTM and conduct experiments to observe the effectiveness of each module. The experimental results are shown in Table 4. We can get the following observations:

1) Removing the Fasttext module, the F1-score is basically unchanged, but the inference time increases by 110%. This demonstrates that using Fasttext network for preliminary classification can reduce the overall inference time and improve the interaction efficiency of the whole system.

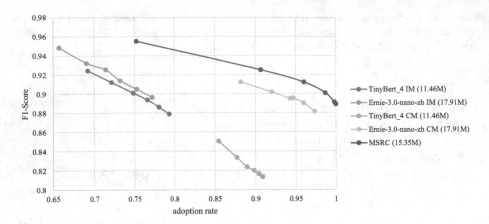

Fig. 3. The interception rate and F1-Score of CFTM and baseline models as interception threshold ϕ_0 changes in CHUZHOU dataset.

Table 4. F1-Score and inference time when replacing each module of CFTM.

	CHUZHOU		EIP	
	F1-Score	infer time (ms)	F1-Score	infer time (ms)
CFTM with Fasttext	**0.7840**	**6.6**	**0.8890**	**6.9**
CFTM without Fasttext	0.7804	14.5	0.8816	14.4
CFTM with roformer-sim small	**0.7840**	6.6	**0.8890**	6.9
CFTM with TinyBert$_4$ Chinese	0.7450	**3.2**	0.8684	3.8
CFTM with Ernie-3.0-nano-zh	0.7656	3.7	0.8623	**3.7**
CFTM with optimization	**0.7840**	**6.6**	**0.8890**	**6.9**
CFTM without optimization	0.7610	7.0	0.8600	7.0

2) By replacing Roformer-sim small in CFTM with TinyBert$_4$ Chinese and Ernie-3.0-nano-zh, we can observe that although the overall inference time is reduced by 50%, the F1-score drops by 2 4. This demonstrates that although Roformer-sim increases part of the inference time, it can greatly improve the overall matching success rate, thereby improving the response quality of the customer service question answering.

3) By comparing the roformer-sim model fine-tuned on the training dataset using the loss function proposed in this paper with using the traditional cosine loss function, We can observe that the inference time basically remains the same, but the F1-Score drops by 2 points. This demonstrates that optimizing using the loss function proposed in this paper can effectively improve the matching accuracy of the model and correctly handle more hard-to-classify samples.

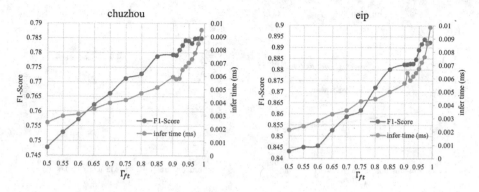

Fig. 4. On CHUZHOU and EIP datasets, when the hyper-parameter γ_{ft} takes different values, the changes of the F1-Score and inference time.

4.7 Hyper-parameters Selection

For the three hyper-parameters γ_{ft}, ϕ_0 and ϕ_1 in CFTM, in this part we constructs related experiments to help choosing appropriate values.

For the interception threshold γ_{ft} of the Fasttext, we took different values from 0.5 to 1 to observe its effect on CFTM. The results are shown in Fig. 4, we can observe that with the increase of γ_{ft}, the F1-Score and inference time show an overall upward trend. However, when γ_{ft} is in the range of 0.9 to 1, the growth of F1-Score tends to be slow, sometimes with a small decrease, while the inference time exponentially increases. Therefore, the suggested value of γ_{ft} given in this paper is 0.85 to 0.95. For all experiments in this paper, we set γ_{ft} to 0.95.

For the threshold ϕ_0, we have given the relevant experiments in the Sect. 4.5, and show its impact on the adoption rate and F1-Score. As ϕ_0 increases, the F1-Score tends to rise, and the adoption rate tends to decline. The actual value of ϕ_0 needs to be determined according to different application scenarios and requirements. If you have more human customer service to process unintercepted data and want the system to have a very high response accuracy, you can set ϕ_0 to a higher value. If there is no requirement for a high response accuracy, and want the system to give as many responses as possible, you can set ϕ_0 lower.

Threshold ϕ_1 mainly determines the number of questions that are given to guide the user when the matching result with the highest similarity given by CFTM is less than ϕ_0. This value will have different effects depending on different datasets. In this paper, we take the EIP and CHUZHOU datasets as examples to show the effect of ϕ_1, the results are shown in Fig. 5. For the CHUZHOU and EIP datasets in this paper, our recommended setting for ϕ_1 is 0.04.

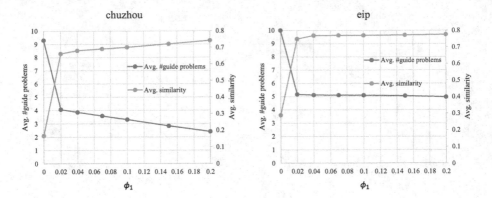

Fig. 5. On the CHUZHOU and EIP datasets, when the hyper-parameter ϕ_1 takes different values and the number of guiding questions given by each input sample is limited to a maximum of 10, the average number of guiding questions given by CFTM and the average similarity of these guide questions to the input samples.

5   Conclusion

In this paper, we mainly discuss the customer service question answering under the condition of limiting the amount of model parameters and computational complexity. we propose **CFTM**, A **C**oarse-to-**F**ine **T**ext **M**atching Framework, which consists of Fasttext coarse-grained classification, and Roformer-sim fine-grained sentence vector matching optimized with CoSENT. In the experimental part, We conduct extensive experiments on CHUZHOU and EIP customer service questioning datasets from KONKA. The result shows that CFTM outperforms baselines across all metrics, achieving a 2.5 improvement in F1-Score and a 30% improvement in inference time, which demonstrates that our CFTM gets higher response accuracy and faster interaction speed in customer service question answering. Meanwhile, we perform ablation analysis to demonstrate the effectiveness of each module of CFTM. Finally, we conduct experiments to measure the impact of each hyper-parameter on CFTM and give appropriate values for each hyper-parameter.

Acknowledgments. We thank all anonymous reviewers for their helpful comments. This work was partially supported by the National Natural Science Foundation of China (62006062, 62176076), Shenzhen Foundational Research Funding JCYJ202 00109113441941, Shenzhen Key Technology Project JSGG20210802154400001, and Joint Lab of HITSZ and Konka.

References

1. Wen, T., Gasic, M., Mrksic, N., Su, P., Vandyke, D., Young, S.J.: Semantically conditioned LSTM-based natural language generation for spoken dialogue systems. The Association for Computational Linguistics (2015)

2. Wang, S., Jiang, J.: A compare-aggregate model for matching text sequences. In: 5th International Conference on Learning Representations, ICLR 2017, Toulon, France, Conference Track Proceedings, OpenReview.net (2017)
3. Huang, P., He, X., Gao, J., Deng, L., Acero, A., Heck, L.P.: Learning deep structured semantic models for web search using clickthrough data. In: ACM (2013)
4. Shen, Y., He, X., Gao, J., Deng, L., Mesnil, G.: Learning semantic representations using convolutional neural networks for web search. In: ACM (2014)
5. Hu, B., Lu, Z., Li, H., Chen, Q.: Convolutional neural network architectures for matching natural language sentences. In: Ghahramani, Z., Welling, M., Cortes, C., Lawrence, N.D., Weinberger, K.Q., eds Advances in Neural Information Processing Systems 27: Annual Conference on Neural Information Processing Systems 2014, pp. 2042–2050. Montreal, Quebec, Canada (2014)
6. Mueller, J., Thyagarajan, A.: Siamese recurrent architectures for learning sentence similarity. In: AAAI Press (2016)
7. Wan, S., Lan, Y., Guo, J., Xu, J., Pang, L., Cheng, X.: A deep architecture for semantic matching with multiple positional sentence representations. In: AAAI Press (2016)
8. Pang, L., Lan, Y., Guo, J., Xu, J., Wan, S., Cheng, X.: Text matching as image recognition. In: AAAI Press (2016)
9. Wang, Z., Hamza, W., Florian, R.: Bilateral multi-perspective matching for natural language sentences (2017)
10. Chen, Q., Zhu, X., Ling, Z., Wei, S., Jiang, H., Inkpen, D.: Enhanced LSTM for natural language inference. Association for Computational Linguistics (2017)
11. Qiao, Y., Xiong, C., Liu, Z., Liu, Z.: Understanding the behaviors of BERT in ranking. CoRR abs/1904.07531 (2019)
12. Devlin, J., Chang, M., Lee, K., Toutanova, K.: BERT: pre-training of deep bidirectional transformers for language understanding. In: Association for Computational Linguistics (2019)
13. Reimers, N., Gurevych, I.: Sentence-BERT: sentence embeddings using siamese BERT-networks. In: Association for Computational Linguistics (2019)
14. Su, J.: Simbertv2 is here! fusion of retrieved and generated Roformer-sim models (In Chinese) (2021)
15. Lu, Z., Li, H.: A deep architecture for matching short texts. In: Burges, C.J.C., Bottou, L., Ghahramani, Z., Weinberger, K.Q., eds Advances in Neural Information Processing Systems 26: 27th Annual Conference on Neural Information Processing Systems 2013. Proceedings of a meeting held, pp. 1367–1375. Lake Tahoe, Nevada, United States (2013)
16. Guo, J., Fan, Y., Ai, Q., Croft, W.B.: A deep relevance matching model for ad-hoc retrieval. In: ACM (2016)
17. Joulin, A., Grave, E., Bojanowski, P., Mikolov, T.: Bag of tricks for efficient text classification. In: Association for Computational Linguistics (2017)
18. Su, J.: Cosent (1): a more efficient sentence vector scheme than sentence-BERT (In Chinese) (2022)
19. Jiao, X., et al.: Tinybert: distilling BERT for natural language understanding. Volume EMNLP 2020 of Findings of ACL. In: Association for Computational Linguistics (2020)
20. Sun, Y., et al.: ERNIE 3.0: large-scale knowledge enhanced pre-training for language understanding and generation. CoRR abs/2107.02137 (2021)

Deep Learning-Based Visual Defect Inspection System for Pouch Battery Packs

Xu Wang$^{(\boxtimes)}$ and Pan Cheng

Sankyo Precision (Huizhou) Co., Ltd., Huizhou, China
wdx04@outlook.com

Abstract. Every year, billions of pouch battery packs are produced worldwide. The production of pouch battery packs has been highly automated. However, visual inspection is the last step of production that still requires a large number of workers. We present the hardware and software design of an automated visual inspection system for pouch battery packs. We have achieved a 4% false alarm rate, 0.7% missing alarm rate, and 3.5 s cycle time on this challenging task through well-designed optical hardware and the latest deep learning techniques.

Keywords: Machine vision · Defect inspection · Image processing · Deep learning · Semantic segmentation · ConvNext

1 Introduction

A pouch battery pack is a battery packaging format that is well known for the efficient use of space and achieves a 90 to 95% packaging efficiency, the highest among battery packs. Today, Lithium polymer pouch battery packs are widely used in smartphones, and they can also be found in applications in other consumer, military and automotive industries (Fig. 1).

Fig. 1. A pouch battery pack

Visual defect inspection of pouch battery packs is one of the most challenging tasks in industrial machine vision:

- Pouch battery packs are not standardized. Every model has its own structure and list of defect types
- Typically, a pouch battery model has 40 or more different defect types, leading to high software complexity
- Pouch battery packs may have parts with vastly different optical properties (reflective/dark/transparent), making it hard to design the imaging scheme
- Pouch battery packs have no metal shell, their corners are more susceptible to damage, and extra care is required when handling the corners, meaning more data to process
- Identification of a few defect types may require human interaction, for example, touching the product surface to estimate the depth of an indentation.

We initially planned to develop the visual defect inspection equipment for pouch battery packs in 2018. But the development was delayed until late 2021 when we found a good imaging scheme.

2 Hardware Design

Our machine vision hardware consists of two high-performance industrial computers, one microcontroller board, 12 monochrome cameras, and 22 lighting sources powered by two 12-channel light controllers. Cameras and Lights are arranged as three types of inspection stations:

- **FPC Station ($\times$1)**: $2\times$ 5.0 MP camera, $2\times$ Square Coaxial Light to inspect defects in the top and bottom sides of the Flexible Printed Circuit (FPC) connector.
- **Top Station ($\times$1)**: $1\times$ 8.8 MP camera, $1\times$ Diffused Square Light, $4\times$ Bar Light to inspect battery body defects from the top side. All the bar lights are oriented horizontally.
- **Bottom & Edge Station ($\times$3)**: $3\times$ 8.8 MP cameras, $1\times$ Diffused Square Light, and $4\times$ Bar Light to inspect battery body defects from the bottom side, edges, and corners. The workload of this station is much higher than the other two stations, so we have three parallel Bottom-Edge stations to reduce the cycle time to 3.5 s (Figs. 2 and 3).

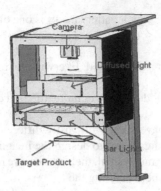

Fig. 2. Camera and lights placement of the top station

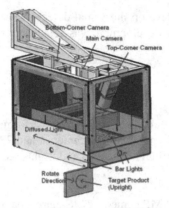

Fig. 3. Cameras and lights placement of bottom-edge station

The microcontroller board is the heart of the machine vision system. It receives trigger signals from the equipment's master control system (PLC), operates the cameras and lights with a programmed timing sequence, notifies industrial computers to receive images from industrial cameras and process them, and finally transfers the processing results back to PLC (Fig. 4).

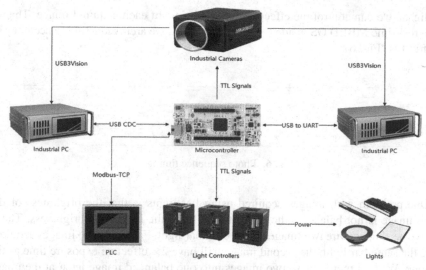

Fig. 4. Hardware connection map

3 Image Acquisition

The microcontroller board software controls the image acquisition process by synchronizing signals to cameras and light controllers.

The FPC station is relatively easy to deal with, so we will focus on the other two stations.

For the top and bottom surfaces of the battery body, we will take nine images in a row using the main (center) camera, each in different lighting conditions. Firstly we take one shot using the main diffused light. This image is suitable for checking the printing quality on the battery surface. Then we take two shots each with the four bar lights located at the east, north, west, and south side of the product. These images can highlight the uneven places on the battery surface, including scratches, pits, pinholes, bulges, and bumps, because these places will react differently to light in different directions. This is the main strength of our image acquisition system (Fig. 5).

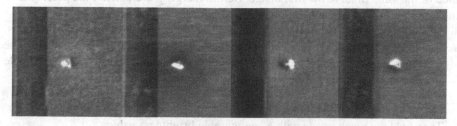

Fig. 5. A pit under different directions of lighting

Cameras are triggered at the rising edge of external signals, and lights are only lit up when their trigger signals are kept HIGH. By scheduling the overlapping time of cameras and lights, we can control the effective exposure time of each acquired image. Thanks to the real-time MBED OS inside the microcontroller, we archived a timing accuracy of roughly 1us (Fig. 6).

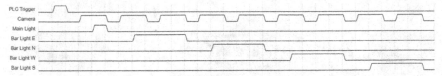

Fig. 6. Photo sequence timing

One problem with images acquired using bar lights is that the brightness of the whole image is not balanced: the closer to the light, the higher the brightness. That's why we need to acquire two images using each bar light. For every two images acquired using the same bar light, the second image will have 2× effective exposure time as the first one. We will merge these two images into one balanced image later, at the image preprocessing stage.

After acquiring the image of the bottom side, we lift the product up-right to process one of its edges. Then we rotate the product 45 × 7 times to process the other three edges and four corners in order. Only bar lights are used when processing edges and corners. For each edge, we take six shots using the main camera (no need to take two shots for Bar Light N and S because of the short relative distance). For each corner, the main and two corner-only cameras take one shot for each bar light, making up 12 images in total.

4   Balancing the Bar Light Images

The brightness of images acquired using the bar lights is unbalanced, with over-exposed and dark sides. We need to balance these images before we can apply standard image-processing algorithms to them.

Firstly, we merge the two images acquired using the same bar light. The method is simple: since we know the second image is 2× as bright as the first one, we replace all overexposure pixels (255 for unsigned 8 bit data) in the second image with 2× the value of the same pixel in the first image. Before merging, we convert the pixel data to single-precision floating-point numbers to prevent arithmetic overflow.

Secondly, we merge the four images acquired using bar lights of different directions. We assume the largest connected component of the surface should have roughly the same brightness. So, for all pixels inside that connected component, we should be able to calculate their "preferred" brightness value:

1. Calculate a pixel-by-pixel mean brightness image from all four images
2. Threshold the mean image with a configurable brightness value
3. Find the largest connected component in the binary image generated by the previous step
4. Calculate the mean value of all pixels of the mean image, masked by the largest connected component, which is the "preferred" brightness value.

By getting the preferred brightness value, we can calculate a multiplier for each pixel inside the connected component, where:

```
current value * multiplier= preferred value.
```

Now we have a multiplier image for each bar light image, though only part of the pixels has a known multiplier value, and the already-known multiplier values are highly noisy. We need to remove noises from the multiplier images and ensure every pixel in the multiplier images has a value:

1. Remove the outstanding noises by applying a 5×5 median blur filter
2. For each unknown pixel in multiplier images, assign it the value of the nearest known pixel
3. Blur the multiplier images with a large 255×255 Gaussian kernel

We get four balanced images by multiplying the four bar light images with their corresponding multiplier images. We merge the four balanced images into one four-channel image. The four-channel image is packed with rich information and will be used to feed our neural network models.

5   The Defect Detection Pipeline

After merging the bar light images, we now have one diffused light image and one merged bar light image. We will put these images into the defect detection pipeline (Fig. 7):

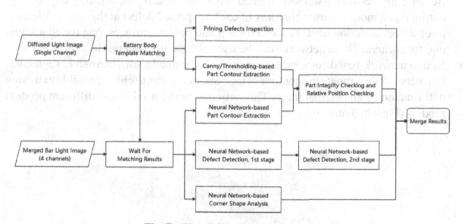

Fig. 7. The defect detection pipeline

The first step in the defect detection pipeline is battery body template matching. This gives us a rough outer contour of the product, the coordinate of its center and corners, so we can calculate the region-of-interests (ROIs) for the following steps and filter out any false defect responses generated from background noises.

After template matching, we can do five more image-processing tasks in parallel:

1. Printing Defects Inspection: there are several types of defects in printing quality, such as incomplete print, distorted print, and blurred print. Inspecting such defects is done by splitting the printing content into many small blocks, then matching every block against a master template and computing the differences.
2. Canny/Thresholding-based part contour extraction: for parts with conspicuous separation from their surroundings, we can binarize the image ROI by a specific grayscale threshold and extract the part contour from the binary image. Alternatively, we can apply a Canny edge detector to the image ROI and find the part contour by pattern matching.
3. Neural network-based part contour extraction: A semantic segmentation network is used to detect the contours of parts with inconspicuous separation from their surroundings. There are three networks of such type in our system, one for the top surface, one for the bottom surface, and one for the front edge. These networks are product model specific.
4. Neural network-based defect detection: a semantic segmentation network can detect abnormal pixels directly. Detectable defect types include dirty, foreign objects, folds, scratches, bubbles, indentations, dents, pinholes, leakage of electrolytes, and other damages. Similar defects are combined into one class in the neural network to make the training process faster. In 1st stage, we feed the network with one large image ROI covering the whole battery surface, defects detected at this stage are regarded as "suspected defects." We record the central position of each suspected defect to verify them at the next stage. In 2nd stage, we create 256×256 patches around the central position of suspected defects and feed the network with these patches. Because the network itself was trained with 256×256 patches, it is expected to output much more accurate contours of each suspected defect at this stage. We have three defect detection networks, one for top and bottom surfaces, one for edges, and one for corners. These networks can be used across different product models.
5. Neural network-based corner shape analysis: we trained a small semantic segmentation network to compute the contour of the battery corners to check possible extrusion deformation by an external force. This network can be used across different product models (Figs. 8, 9 and 10).

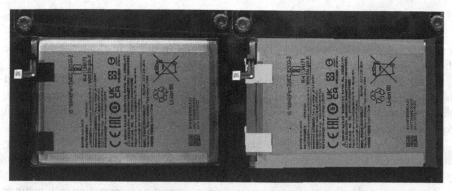

Fig. 8. Top surface image and position labels

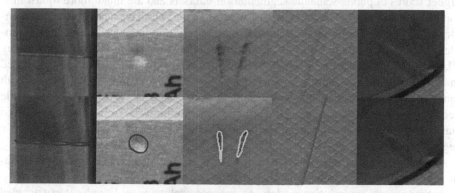

Fig. 9. Sample defects and labels

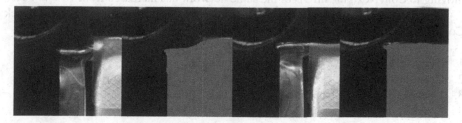

Fig. 10. Deformed corner and normal corner

For edge/corner without the diffused light image, we use one of the channels in the merged bar light image for body template matching and ignore all the steps that would use the diffused light image.

Once the contours of each part are obtained, we can check their integrity and detect position shifts, skews, and unexpected overlaps between parts.

As shown in Fig. 7, we merge the results of the four branches into the final result and send the result to the microcontroller.

6   Enhanced Segmentation Network: From GCN to ConvNext

Semantic segmentation networks play a crucial role in our defect-detection pipeline. Their accuracy determines the entire system's performance.

Since 2017 we have used customized Global Convolution Network (GCN) [1] models in several of our machine vision software, including inspection software for ring magnets, laser welding points, and areca nuts. In most cases, our GCN models meet our requirements of accuracy, robustness, speed, and ease of deployment.

But for a more complex problem like direct defect detection for top/bottom battery surfaces, our GCN-based model stopped making progress after reaching a mean IOU of 78%, which is not enough to archive our goal.

Then we started looking for more contemporary semantic segmentation architectures. Most notably, Vision Transformer (ViTs)-based [2] models like SegFormer [3] archived higher scores at public semantic segmentation datasets and are much more robust than traditional Convolution-based models. Unfortunately, ViTs have a computational complexity of $O(N^2)$. SegFormer introduced some speed optimizations to reduce the complexity, but it is still more than $10\times$ slower than our GCN-based model when processing a large 3072×2048 image. Another option is ConvNext [4], a new Convolution-based image classification network to compete with ViTs. ConvNcxt improved on ResNet with many minor modifications, some of which are borrowed from ViT-based models while keeping the linear computing complexity of Convolution Nets. ConvNext also showed state-of-the-art performance on public datasets when used as the backbone for semantic segmentation.

Thanks to the great deep learning framework PyTorch [5], and the tremendous semantic segmentation toolkit mmsegmentation [6], we can quickly get started with ConvNext and other recent segmentation models. After some evaluation on ConvNext, we decided to replace GCN with it for all semantic segmentation models used in our system. By moving to ConvNext, the mIOU of the same network has increased from 78% to 85%.

To reduce memory usage and increase inference speed, we modified the stock ConvNext + UperNet model with the following changes:

1. ConvNext backbone's depth is reduced to [1, 3].
2. ConvNext backbone's channels are reduced to [8, 16, 32, 64] or [16, 32, 64, 128].
3. UperNet decoder's channels are reduced to 32 or 64.
4. UperNet decoder's pooling sizes are changed to [1, 2, 4] or [1, 2, 4, 8].

The resulting models have only 200K or 800K params but still, provide good segmentation accuracy.

The networks that directly detect defects use the 800k params model. They are trained with randomly cropped 256×256 patches from source images.

The networks that find part contours use the 200k params model. They are trained with randomly cropped 1536×1024 patches from half-size source images.

The network that analyzes the corner shape also uses the 200k params model. It's trained with randomly cropped 256×256 patches from source images.

The mm segmentation framework is slightly modified to support 4-channel input images (Table 1).

Table 1. Training configuration and results

Network model	Patch size	Classes	Batch size	Batch time	mIOU
Top/Bottom defects	256 × 256	4	192	0.34 s/RTX3080Ti	85.62
Edge defects	256 × 256	5	384	0.86 s/RTX2080Ti	95.02
Corner defects	256 × 256	4	192	0.35 s/RTX3080Ti	93.64
Top parts	1536 × 1024	6	16	1.28 s/RTX2080Ti	98.45
Bottom parts	1536 × 1024	3	16	0.73 s/RTX3080Ti	98.58
Front edge parts	384 × 256	3	256	0.60 s/RTX3080Ti	93.47
Corner shape	256 × 256	2	384	0.7 9 s/RTX2080Ti	98.87

We use ONNX Runtime [7] to execute the trained models on our industrial computers. ONNX Runtime supports GPU acceleration through a variety of Execution Providers. We tested the inference latency of the most time-consuming defect detection network against a few different GPUs and EPs. The CUDA EP runs faster than the DirectML EP, but the DirectML EP uses much less video memory (1.7 GB) than the CUDA EP (4 GB). We chose the DirectML EP for production use and equipped each computer with an NVIDIA RTX3070 GPU (Table 2).

Table 2. Inference Latency for different GPUs and Execution Providers

GPU model	Execution provider	Inference latency
NVIDIA RTX3080Ti	DirectML	113 ms
NVIDIA RTX2080Ti	CUDA	151 ms
NVIDIA RTX2080Ti	DirectML	167 ms
NVIDIA RTX3070	DirectML	165 ms
NVIDIA GTX1070	DirectML	233 ms
AMD RX5500XT	DirectML	328 ms
Intel Arc A380	DirectML	370 ms

7 Experimental Results

By the end of October 2022, our equipment was trialed at the customer's site for two months, and an average of 600 new products were checked by our inspection system per day at a cycle time of 3.5 s. Human inspectors then rechecked these products to calculate our system's false alarm rate and the missing alarm rate. During the trial period, our false alarm rate decreased from 15% to 4%, and our missing alarm rate decreased from 3% to 0.7%. Products that were falsely reported are mainly those with dirt or pits but are considered acceptable by human inspectors. There is no problem detecting common types of defects. It shows that the quality of our acquired images and the effectiveness of our neural network models are good. The NG products that failed to be detected belonged to some rarely seen defect types for which we hadn't collected enough training samples. We are continuing to improve our inspection system further to reduce the missing alarm rate to below 0.3%, as our customer requires.

## 8	Conclusion

We proved it is possible to inspect the visual defects of pouch battery packs with industrial cameras and deep learning technology.

We have several of the largest customers in the Li-Polymer pouch battery packs industry, with more than 500 production lines. With some modifications, we can extend our inspection system to support semi-finished pouch battery cells, which is also a large market. Our inspection system can effectively reduce four inspectors for each of our customer's production lines. Compared to human inspectors, our inspection system is more consistent in terms of testing standards, thus will improve product quality.

There are still some problems yet to be solved. We will investigate these problems in the future:

- About half of our neural networks are bound to a specific product model. Every time we want to support a new product model, we will have to train new neural networks, which takes manpower and time. We will accelerate product changeovers with more flexible neural networks.
- A few defects are barely visible in the images taken from 2D cameras. For example, small bumps under a thick adhesive paper are hard to detect. We may use an additional 3D camera to solve this problem.

References

1. Peng, C., Zhang, X., Yu, G., Luo, G., Sun, J.: Large Kernel matters —— improve semantic segmentation by global convolutional network. arXiv:1703.02719(2017)
2. Dosovitskiy, A.: An image is worth 16x16 words: transformers for image recognition at scale. arXiv:2010.11929 (2020)
3. Xie, E., et al.: SegFormer: simple and efficient design for semantic segmentation with transformers. arXiv 2105.15203(2021)
4. Liu, Z., et al.: A ConvNet for the 2020s. arXiv:2201.03545 (2022)
5. PyTorch Homepage, https://pytorch.org/. Accessed 30 Oct 2022
6. mmsegmentation Homepage. https://github.com/open-mmlab/mmsegmentation. Accessed 30 Oct 2022
7. ONNX Runtime Homepage. https://onnxruntime.ai/. Accessed 30 Oct 2022

Variant Mixed Integer Linear Programming Model for Merchandises Optimization in Fast-Moving Consumer Goods Industry

Yang He[✉], Huiqin Zeng, Lu Peng, and Yishuang Ning

Kingdee Research, Kingdee International Software Group Company Limited, Wan Chai, China
y_h@kingdee.com

Abstract. With the continuous development of economic globalization and the spread of the new crown epidemic, enterprises face more intense market competition and insufficient market share. Companies in the fast-moving consumer goods (FMCG) industry must continuously improve their profitability and profitability. In a series of processes such as "production", "sales" and "new product research and development", the company's efficiency is improved, costs are reduced, and the core competitiveness of the company is formed. To address the issues such as enterprise cost input, capital allocation and production decision, we utilize a variant mixed integer linear programming model to establish decision rules and apply the analysis and quantification methods to make overall arrangements for the limited resources in the economic management system, such as human, financial and merchandise. We also provide scientific quantitative basis and sustainable solutions for enterprise management decision makers.

Keywords: Mixed integer linear programming model · Merchandises optimization · Decision rules

1 Introduction

Improving efficiency is an indispensable requirement of people in economics, transportation, production, and other activities [1].

During World War II, modern operations research played an important role in the battlefield. Until the end of World War II, the world economy began to recover, and operation research was also widely used in finance, production, and other fields; accordingly, its branches developed. In the 1990s, with the rapid development of computer science, the range of problems to be solved continued to expand, and the application scope of operations research achieved revolutionary breakthroughs. In the 21st century, the advent of the big data era established a bigger stage for operations research. How to transform big data into optimal decision-making in modern commercial production and distribution environments has become a key subject and an important part of operations research [2]. Optimization decisions in this regard, including the correct choice of construction locations, transportation modes and routes, and maximum and minimum inventory management policies can significantly improve system performance. It was found that over 380 articles published in the ISI and Web of Science databases between 2005–2016 applied techniques from advanced O.R. SCN optimization research [15]. Global companies (e.g., China) face numerous problems in product delivery, resource allocation, and inventory management optimization. The viability of a company largely depends on the ability to produce excellent products at a highly low cost [20]. Ezema and Amakom [21] asserted that companies around the world are challenged by the scarcity of product delivery and high reliance on expert experience, which can lead to low sales, long delivery times from central warehouses, and increased warehouse costs. Companies must create a technology that helps them excel at controlling costs and evenly distributing resources. The profits of Apparel manufacturing companies were significantly affected by production costs and resource costs [16]. Linear programming is a technique and model for operations research, which is used to control the cost of the company effectively, allocate the best production resources, and plan the best path. It is currently the most widely used optimization technique and scheme on the market [17]. Different products and production lines require different costs and resource inputs at different production stages. Therefore, the Linear Programming Problem (LPP) technique will be used to maximize the sales profit and minimize the cost of the product mix within a specific time. This is the best-performing method for selecting the best practical solution to satisfy the specified objective function subject to various business constraints among all scenarios [22]. As stated by Reeb and Leavengood [18], it is a planning process that allocates various resources (e.g., manpower, raw materials, machines, and money) in an optimal mathematical formula so that costs can be kept at a minimum level, and sales profits are maximized. However, LPP can also be problematic in allocating a large number of high-quality resources to certain products in a way that maximizes sales profits and minimizes control costs [23]. However, for company employees who are not familiar with the technology, there will be a huge gap in using LPP techniques to allocate resources to product lines and quantitative analysis of each product lead time.

To address these issues, we proposed a variant hybrid linear programming model to optimize the distribution of bread and maximize profits over time series cycles. Specifically, it first used a power-law analysis [24] to observe data distribution and cluster data to prolong the life cycle of commodities, thereby improving the stationarity of time series data. In addition, commodities with high similarity are captured by Brich clustering algorithm. Moreover, experiments in bakeries demonstrated the effectiveness and agility of our proposed method.

2   Merchandises Optimization Based on Variant Mixed Integer Linear Programming Model

Bakery company fresh delivery models need to be optimized, mainly covering Shenyang, Dalian, Changchun, and southern cities in China. The main products are short-and medium-term bread. For policy makers, how to determine the distribution of each merchandise to meet the sales needs of the store and minimize the final return rate (minimum) to achieve a win-win situation for sales and returns are two important problems. In this paper, variant mixed integer linear programming (VMILP) [5] model is used to address these problems.

2.1   Variant Mixed Integer Linear Programming Model

Like establishing a mathematical model, building variant mixed integer linear programming model from business problems has the following steps [3, 4]:

- Define the decision variables according to the business requirements and database analysis;
- Define the constraints that satisfy the decision variables;
- Define the objective function through the relationship between the decision variables and the objective function.

The characteristics of the defined variant mixed integer linear programming model are as follows:

- The model has many decision variables (s_1, s_2, s_3, … …, s_n), where n is the number of decision variables. The values of a set of decision variables can represent an array, while the decision variables are non-negative;
- The decision variables in the objective function are all linear data. According to specific business problems, the task of the model to maximize or minimize the objective function based on the constraints;
- Similarly, the decision variables in the constraints are also linear.

In this case, the variant mixed integer linear programming model can be regarded as a linear programming model [14], and its objective functions are all linear functions. In order to optimize decision variables (s_n), the constraints can be equality or inequality.

2.2   Business Process

For business process, we first introduce business data from the hive database [19], and choose the corresponding analysis method through the business form. The industry generally adopts analysis method through a mainline logic, with top-bottom order.

The main purposes of analyzing the data are in the following:

- Provide data support for subsequent model selection;
- Find out the real maximum and minimum values, in order to ensure the accuracy of the constrains.

Figure 1 shows the whole business process, including data preparation, data filtering, data processing, data analysis, solution selection, model calculation, value optimization.

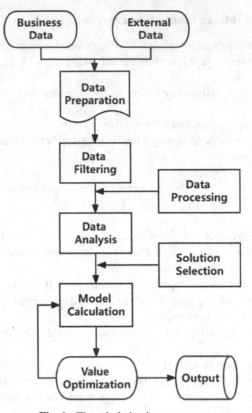

Fig. 1. The whole business process

2.3 Methodology

The data collection procedure was quantitative in nature and relied on daily modifications by the case company's salesperson to finalize the concepts relevant to the resources held and consumed and the each loaf delivery quantity. The declaration of each component is as follows:

- VARIABLES is the set of decision variables in a VMILP model. According to the historical data of the bakery company from 2020 to 2022:
    OC_i is the delivery quantity of bread;
    RC_i is the return of bread;
    sale is the total sale of the all bread sales price;
- SCALARS in VMILP model is used to declare or initialize the constant term. In order to meet the needs of bakery shops:
    OC_per_i is the unit price of bread delivered;
    RC_per_i is the return unit price of bread;
    S is the historical daily sales of bread;
    $FCQY_i$ is the inventory quantity of bread;
    $NFCQY_i$ is the next inventory quantity of bread;

- PLAN is used as a solution in the VMILP model. After investigation, the bread return rate in bakeries is ideally no more than 6%. But the reality will always happen more than 6%, so according to the business data, the return rate is divided into three solutions, solution-1, solution-2, solution-3. The following Table 1 gives a summary of all solutions.

Table 1. Return rate for the bread solutions

	Solution-1	Solution-2	Solution-3
Return rate	6%	10%	20%

Finally, the constraints and the objective function of the VMILP model are as follows:

1. Total sale price of the all bread sales

   The total sales of the bakery includes the delivery quantity of bread, the return of bread, unit price of bread, return unit price of bread, inventory quantity of bread, and the next inventory quantity of bread. Therefore, the equation of the total sale of the bakery is expressed as follows:

$$z = MAX \sum_{i \in I} S\_per_i * (OC_i + FCQY_i - NFCQY_i - RC_i) \qquad (1)$$

2. The constraint equation of total sale of the all bread sales

   According to the requirements of the solution, the total sales cannot exceed S (it must not be negative), so the constraint equation for the sales volume is expressed as follows:

$$0 \le \sum_{i \in I} (OC_i + FCQY_i - NFCQY_i - RC_i) \le S_{max} \qquad (2)$$

3. The constraint equation of the daily delivery quantity of bread

   According to the requirements of the solution, the daily delivery quantity cannot exceed the historical maximum data (it must not be negative), so the constraint equation for the daily delivery quantity is expressed as follows:

$$OC_{min} \le \sum_{i \in I} OC_i \le OC_{max} \qquad (3)$$

4. The constraint equation of the return rate of the solution

   According to the requirements of the solution, each constraint equation represents a solution for the return rate is expressed as follows:

$$Solution - 1 = RC_i \le \sum_{i \in I} OC_i * 6\% \qquad (4)$$

Further expand:

$$Solution - 2 = RC_i \le \sum_{i \in I} OC_i * 10\% \qquad (5)$$

$$Solution - 3 = RC_i \le \sum_{i \in I} OC_i * 20\% \qquad (6)$$

3 Experimental Result

3.1 Experimental Setup

Data Set. To evaluate the effectiveness of the VMILP model, we use the 2020 to 2022 by bakeries dataset. The null values and error values about 300 through preprocessing and filtering. In this work, we determined the correct upper and lower bounds through cluster analysis [6], merchandise similarity analysis [7], merchandise life cycle analysis [8], merchandise average sales interval analysis [9].

Experimental Method. Mark each merchandise by finding the similarity through Euclidean distance [10]. Dataset is clustered through the Brich cluster algorithm [11], found out the best cluster is calculated through the CH evaluation metrics [12], and finally reclassified and saved.

Hypothetical Test. In order to prove that the clustered data is better than the original data, the *p-value* of the filtered cluster data and the original data is calculated by ADF method [13]. After comparison, it's found out the clustered data is more stationary than the original data in the time series.

3.2 Computational Results of the Total Sales

According to each analysis method and different solution, we can get different optimization delivery quantity of merchandises and total sales through computational results. Figure 2 shows the optimization results by utilizing the VMILP model with different solutions.

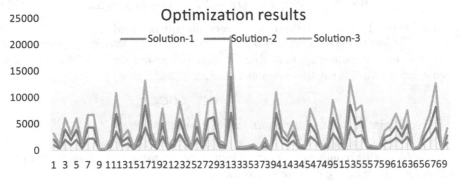

Fig. 2. The optimization results of VMILP model with different solutions.

Table 2 shows the optimization results through different solution. From this table, we can draw the following conclusions: 1) the total sales decrease with the return rate of the solution; 2) Solution-1 with the lowest return rate achieves the highest total sales. The reason might be that when $i = 1, 2, 3$ we get different solutions and different constraints. The most important thing about the mixed integer linear programming model is to obtain

Table 2. The comparison of different solutions

	Total sales (yuan)
Solution-1 (6%)	¥329,851
Solution-2 (10%)	¥329,727
Solution-3 (20%)	¥329,258

different results through different constraints. Each constraint can be changed into a contour line, when all constraints are change into many contour line can be calculated the feasible region and feasible base.

3.3 Discussion

The prediction model needs a large of historical data as input in the FMCG, and has various factors including seasons, holidays, weather and other trends that can affect the accuracy of the model. Variant mixed integer linear programming model is no need for a large of historical data can get the optimization results. But the engineers must be familiar with the business and make constraints in the model. If engineers have constraints and objective functions, they can make a linear programming modeling solution. It can solve the unicity and the agility of predictive model.

4 Conclusion

This paper proposes an operational optimization solution based on variant mixed integer linear programming model in FMCG industry. In this solution, we use the variant mixed integer linear programming model to find out the correct constraints upper and lower bounds through the bakery historical dataset. Experimental results demonstrate the effectiveness of our proposed method and show variety of results. Our future work will be committed to using variant mixed integer linear programming model for different scenes.

References

1. Dantzig, G.B.: Linear Programming and Extensions. Princeton University Press, Princeton (1963)
2. Wu, J., Ge, X.: Optimization research of generation investment based on linear programming model physics. Procedia **24**, Part B, 1400–1405 (2012)
3. Zhu, L., et al.: Comparison of stochastic programming and linear programming application in animal feed formulation. J. Anhui Agri. Sci. **34**(9), 1778~1779 (2006)
4. Xun, F-f., Ge Y-j., Ma J-y.: Application the linear programme to calculate water environmental capacity. J. Water Resour. Water Eng. **20**(5), 180~183 (2009)
5. Kasilingam, R.G., Lee, C.P.: Selection of vendors — a mixed-integer programming approach. Comput. Ind. Eng. **31**(1–2), 347–350 (1996). ISSN: 0360-8352

6. Tvaronavičienė, M., Razminienė, K., Piccinetti, L.: Aproaches towards cluster analysis. Econ. Sociol. **8**(1), 19–27 (2015)
7. Cheng, T.Y., Wang, S.: A novel approach to clustering merchandise records. J. Comput. Sci. Technol. **22**, 228–231 (2007). https://doi.org/10.1007/s11390-007-9029-3
8. Park, J., Waqar, Z.: Life cycle assessment of returnable mailers used for apparel electronic commerce: a case study in Canada. Packag. Technol. Sci. **35**(9), 651–662 (2022). https://doi.org/10.1002/pts.2653
9. Arunraj, N.S., Ahrens, D.: A hybrid seasonal autoregressive integrated moving average and quantile regression for daily food sales forecasting. Int. J. Prod. Econ. **170**, Part A, 321–335 (2015). ISSN:0925–5273
10. Elmore, K.L., Richman, M.B.: Euclidean distance as a similarity metric for principal component analysis. Monthly Weather Rev. **129**(3), 540–549 (2001)
11. Zhang, T., Ramakrishnan, R., Livny, M.: BIRCH: an efficient data clustering method for very large databases. SIGMOD Rec. **25**(2) 103–114 (1996)
12. Caliński, T., Harabasz, J.: A dendrite method for cluster analysis. Commun. Stat. Theory Methods **3**, 1–27 (1974)
13. Mushtaq, R.: Augmented Dickey Fuller Test. 17August 2011. SSRN: https://ssrn.com/abstract=1911068 or https://doi.org/10.2139/ssrn.1911068
14. Dantzig, G.: Linear programming. Oper. Res. **50**(1), 42–47 (2002). https://doi.org/10.1287/opre.50.1.42.17798
15. Pourhejazy, P., Kwon, O.K.: The new generation of operations research methods in supply chain optimization: a review. Sustainability **8**(10), 1033 (2016). https://doi.org/10.3390/su8101033
16. Arefayne, D., Pal, A.: Productivity improvement through lean manufacturing tools: a case study on Ethiopian garment industry. Int. J. Eng. Res. Technol. **3**(9), 1037–1045 (2014)
17. Reeb, J., Leavengood, S.: Using the Simplex Method to Solve Linear Programming Maximization Problems. Oregon State University, Extension Service (1998)
18. Altman, D., Bland, M.: The normal distribution. BMJ **1995**, 298 (1995)
19. Thusoo, A., et al.: Hive: a warehousing solution over a map-reduce framework. Proc. VLDB Endow. **2**(2), 1626–1629 (2009). https://doi.org/10.14778/1687553.1687609
20. Kumar, V.: JIT based quality management: concepts and implications in Indian context. Int. J. Eng. Sci. Technol. **2**(1), 40–50 (2010)
21. Ezema, B.I., Amakoml, U.: Optimizing profit with the linear programming model: a focus on golden plastic industry limited, Enugu, Nigeria. Interdiscipl. J. Res. Bus. **2**(2), 37–49 (2012)
22. Shaheen, S., Ahmad, T.: Linear programming based optimum resource utilization for manufacturing of electronic toys. Int. Res. J. Eng. Technol. **2**(1), 261–264 (2015)
23. Yahya, W.B.: Determination of optimum product mix at minimum raw material cost, using linear programming. Nigeria J. Pure Appl. Sci. **19**, 1712–1721 (2004)
24. Shatnawi, R., Althebyan, Q.: An empirical study of the effect of power law dis-tribution on the interpretation of OO metrics. Int. Schol. Res. Notices **2013**, 198937, 18 p (2013). https://doi.org/10.1155/2013/198937

Short Paper Track

Automated Data Mapping Based on FastText and LSTM for Business Systems

Zhibin Liu[✉] and Huijun Hu

Kingdee Research, Kingdee International Software Group Company Limited, Shenzhen, China
zhib_liu@kingdee.com

Abstract. With the continuous development of information technology, massive information processing has become an important problem in business systems. However, the metadata information from different business systems lacks a unified and standardized description method. Mapping data by the manual way greatly reduces the efficiency. Therefore, an automated data mapping method is very necessary. In this paper, we regard data mapping as a text classification problem based on the following reasons: 1) the text classification technology has become more and more mature in the field of the natural language processing (NLP), which is very suitable for processing massive data; 2) a large number of heterogeneous mapping data can be treated as text. In order to implement automated data mapping, in this paper, we propose a classification model based on FastText and long-short term memory (LSTM) for data mapping in business systems. By observing the characteristics of mapping data in business systems, we firstly use FastText to learn word representation containing semantic information, and then adopt the LSTM model to extract features for text classification automatically. Experimental results show that the proposed method can automatically classify mapping data in business systems with common quality.

Keywords: Data mapping · Text classification · FastText · Word vectors · Long short-term memory

1 Introduction

Data mapping involves the process of matching data fields from one database to another [1]. Gradually, business data can be analyzed to gain business insights for decision makers after it is processed by data mapping. Nowadays, data comes from many sources, each of which can define similar data points by thousands of ways. However, with the amount of data and the number of data sources increases, the data mapping process becomes very complex [2]. Therefore, an automated data mapping method is very necessary (Fig. 1).

Natural language processing (NLP) is one of the active research areas of artificial intelligence in recent years. With the recent outstanding breakthroughs in NLP, it has aroused the interest of many researchers. NLP is commonly used to classify text data. In short, text classification refers to classify text data based on its content.

Text representation and the choice of classifier have always been the two major technical difficulties and hot spots for text classification. ZHANG et al. [3] combined a

Y. Yang et al. (Eds.): ICCC 2022, LNCS 13734, pp. 75–82, 2022.
https://doi.org/10.1007/978-3-031-23585-6_7

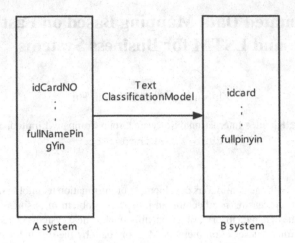

Fig. 1. Automated data mapping method

support vector machine (SVM) with a backpropagation (BP) neural network to classify the input text by using the one-hot representation. Moreover, PACCANARO et al. [4] proposed the concept of distributed representation, commonly known as word embedding, or word vectors. To extract text features better, Kuang et al. [5] improved the term frequency-inverse document frequency (IT-IDF) algorithm and used a naïve Bayesian classifier for text classification. However, those methods cannot extract context-sensitive word vectors. Although Zhang X et al. [6] classified Vietnamese text based on the N-gram statistical language model, which represents text based on the probability that each word appears in front of the n words, while the N-gram model cannot model relationships farther away. In order to solve the problem of the N-gram model to a certain extent, BENGIO et al. [7] proposed the use of neural networks to construct language models. Nevertheless, Numerical representation of text in the above methods suffers from problems such as data sparse and large semantic similarity between modeling words, and is limited to the discovery of lexical characteristics and syntactic features. Therefore, Mikolov et al. [8] pointed out that the vectors trained using the tool word2vec are low-dimensional, continuous, and that the semantic similarity between words can be determined by calculating the cosine distance between these vectors [9]. To bring out the best performance of word2vec, LILLEBERG et al. [10] used word2vec to extract semantic features and classify text based on SVMs. However, SVMs are trained more slowly when sample sizes are large. FastText is a word vector computation and text classification tool that Facebook open-sourced in 2016 [11]. It hasn't been much innovation academically. However, its advantages are also very obvious. For text classification tasks, FastText (shallow network) can often achieve accuracy comparable to deep networks, but in training time is many orders of magnitude faster than deep networks.

For sequential inputs, recurrent neural networks (RNNs) can effectively integrate proximity information [12, 13] to complete NLP tasks. The subclass of RNN, LSTM model [14, 15] which makes good use of contextual feature information, and retains the order information of the text has a strong "memory ability". Therefore, it can auto-matically select features, and classify them to avoid the problem of RNN gradient disappearance.

In this paper, we use FastText and LSTM to categorize the business fields of metadata from two different systems. Firstly, FastText is used to train the word vector with semantic information which is based on the mapping data of the mapping scheme. Secondly, the LSTM model is trained to get the complete semantics of the text and classify the text.

2 Related Work

Text classification is one of the important research topics in the field of NLP [16]. In [3], the one-hot representation method is used to represent text as vectors, and solo thermal coding can convert categorical data into a unified number format, which is convenient for machine learning algorithms to process and calculate. By the way, FastText is a simple and efficient open-source text classification model of Facebook, which used a shallow neural network to achieve word2vec and text classification functions. Its effect is similar to the deep network. Therefore, it can have one hundred times improvement by speed because of saving resources. Also, it can be described as an efficient industrial-grade solution [11]. Jun Liang et al. [17] proposed an emotional classification model based on polarity transfer and LSTM. Firstly, in order to capture deeper semantic information, LSTM was extended to a recurrent neural network based on a tree structure. Secondly, the polarity transfer model was introduced through the correlation between words. Lu et al. [18] combined with the significant classification performance of LSTM in affective classification, and proposed an LSTM model for affective classification, which uses three-word phrases as input for vectorization, and adopts LSTM to introduce a phrase factor mechanism. By combing with the eigenvectors of the embedded layer and the LSTM hidden layer, the information extracted from the text is more accurate.

3 Method

Figure 2 shows the overall flow of the proposed method in this paper. Firstly, to obtain local word vector characteristics, the FastText model that considers the global order of all words is used. At the same time, the open-source tool about FastText which uses Hash ingenuity to add a lot of words with n-gram features can make data mapping and storing fast. Secondly, LSTM models that are well suited for the task of classification through their ability to retain and control historical information is adopted to classify mapping data for final text classification. Next, we will introduce the role of the FastText model and LSTM model about this method in great detail.

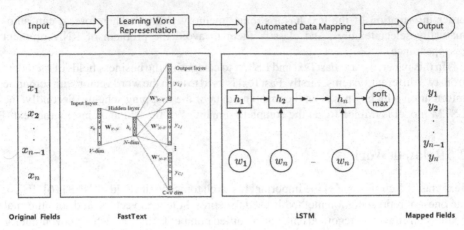

Fig. 2. Overall flow of the proposed method

3.1 Learning Word Representation with FastText

In this paper, we use FastText to obtain word representation for the input text. FastText's main improvement over the original word2vec vector is the inclusion of a character-based n-gram model, which allows the calculation of word representations that do not appear in the training data [20].

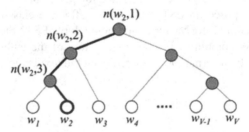

Fig. 3. Huffman Coding Tree in FastText

FastText forms a feature vector of words and phrases in the input layer, and then maps the feature vector to the hidden layer of FastTex through linear transformation, and the hidden layer solves the maximum likelihood function. As shown in Fig. 3, it constructs a Huffman tree according to the weights and model parameters of each category, taking the Huffman Coding tree as the output which is embedding matrix in input layer.

3.2 Classify Mapping Data with LSTM

First of all, in the input layer, there is a sequence vector $X = (x_1, ..x_n)$ with fixed dimension for input. Each row vector is expanded into an m-dimensional vector with each column in X through FastText for the input layer (embedding matrix):

$$A = \begin{pmatrix} a_{1,1} & \cdots & a_{1,k} \\ \vdots & \ddots & \vdots \\ a_{n,1} & \cdots & a_{n,k} \end{pmatrix} \tag{1}$$

where k represents the number of features of the X, which is equivalent to the vector of multidimensional features in each word vector extension layer (Fig. 4).

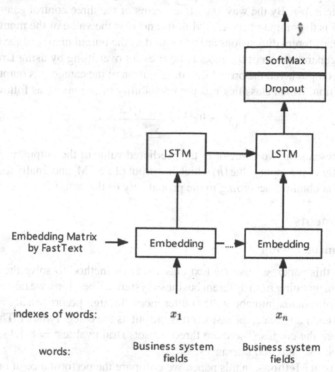

Fig. 4. Automated data mapping with LSTM

As output (w) of input layer which is $X \odot A$, w is also the input of hidden layer. We choose the LSTM model for hidden layer. The LSTM transition functions are defined as follows:

$$i_t = \sigma \left(W_i \cdot \left[h_{t-1}, x_t \right] + b_i \right) \tag{2}$$

$$o_t = \sigma \left(W_o \cdot \left[h_{t-1}, x_t \right] + b_o \right) \tag{3}$$

$$f_t = \sigma \left(W_i \cdot \left[h_{t-1}, x_t \right] + b_f \right) \tag{4}$$

$$C_t = f_t \cdot C_{t-1} + i_t \cdot tanh \left(W_c \cdot \left[h_{t-1}, x_t \right] + b_c \right) \tag{5}$$

$$h_t = o_t \otimes \tanh(C_t) \tag{6}$$

where x is the input data. The number of x is n, which is the number of vectors output by the input layer. The σ and tanh are denoted as the sigmoid activation function *and* the hyperbolic tangent function. The updated value is it and controls the effect of the current data entry on the memory cell state value. Meanwhile, the output gate o_t controls the output of information. In the operating storage unit, the degree of variety of historical information is influenced by the oblivion gate f_t at the last moment. The output gate is W_o. The weight matrix of the input gate is the weight matrix of the input gate. The forgetting gate is W_f. By the way, the offset terms of the three control gates are b_i, b_o, and b_f. The h is the output of the LSTM unit, and C is the value of the memory unit.

In Eq. (6), different dimensions are presented as the output matrix of the LSTM. We improve the generalization of the model and prevent overfitting by using Dropout.

Lastly, in output layer, the probability distribution of the category is output using the softmax function, which classifies x as the probability of category j as follows:

$$P\left(y^i = j|x^i\right) = \frac{v_j v_{x^i}}{\sum_{k=1}^{k} e^{v_j v_{x^i}}} \tag{7}$$

where v_j represents the word vector of the predicted value of the output, v_{x}^i represents the word vector of the input value (h) which is output of LSTM, and finally the prediction label value $\hat{y}$ is obtained according to the probability of the output.

4 Experiments

4.1 Experimental Setup

Data Set. In this paper, we use the text classification method to solve the problem of automatic data mapping from different business systems. Therefore, we take the stitching of multiple form fields into about 4000 utterances through preprocessing and filtering as corpus. In each utterance, the last word is output as the category label. Therefore, we remove it from the corpus. There are three subsets (train:val:test = 8:1:1) by the split corpus. The test set has 400 utterances.

Comparison Methods. In this paper, we compare the performance of our proposed method (FastText + LSTM) with the method that only uses LSTM.

Evaluation Metrics. In all the experiments, we evaluate the classification performance in terms of Precision (P), Recall (R) and F1-measure.

4.2 Experimental Results.

Table 1 Shows the comparison results of our proposed method with other machine learning methods. In Table 1, the final result of the model with FastText is better than the original model, but the results of both experiments are not ideal, and the values of each indicator are low. In many ways, there may be several reasons: 1) too few sentences in the corpus 2) too many labels for classification, and because the classification is based on mapped fields, field mappings between every two different systems produce multiple kinds of labels. In this paper, the total classification labels of the corpus are close to 2,000, however, the total training data is only 3200.

Table 1. Comparison of Precision, Recall and F1-measure results on the test set (metadata from different business systems)

Model	Precision	Recall	F1-measure
LSTM	54.76	54.79	54.31
LSTM + FastText	**55.84**	**55.87**	**55.41**

5 Conclusion

In this paper, our main goal is to use simple machine learning methods to verify the adaptability of business mapping data in text classification models. Specifically, we firstly use FastText to get word representation and then adopt LSTM for simple text classification. Although the accuracy of the final model is low, it can be shown that the word vector matrix added to FastText can optimize model performance and adapt to the data mapping of metadata. Our future work will be committed to text classification model based on FastText and Convolutional Neural Networks (CNN).

Acknowledgements. This paper is supported by the Shenzhen Development and Reform Commission subject (XMHT20200105010).

References

1. El-Sappagh, S.H.A., Hendawi, A.M.A., El Bastawissy, A.H.: A proposed model for data warehouse ETL processes. J. King Saud Univ.-Comput. Inf. Sci. **23**(2), 91–104 (2011)
2. Sreemathy, J., Nisha, S., Gokula, P.R.M.: Data integration in ETL using TALEND. In: 2020 6th International Conference on Advanced Computing and Communication Systems (ICACCS), pp. 1444–1448. IEEE (2020)
3. Zhang, W., Tang, X., Yoshida, T.: Text classification with support vector machine and back propagation neural network. In: Shi, Y., van Albada, G.D., Dongarra, J., Sloot, P.M.A. (eds.) Computational Science – ICCS 2007. ICCS 2007. Lecture Notes in Computer Science, vol. 4490. Springer, Heidelberg (2007). https://doi.org/10.1007/978-3-540-72590-9_21
4. Paccanaro, A., Hinton, G.E.: Learning distributed representations of concepts using linear relational embedding. IEEE Trans. Knowl. Data Eng. **13**(2), 232–244 (2001)
5. Kuang, Q., Xu, X.: Improvement and application of TF•IDF method based on text classification. In: 2010 International Conference on Internet Technology and Applications, pp. 1–4. IEEE (2010)
6. Zhang, X., Wu, B.: Short text classification based on feature extension using the n-gram model. In: 2015 12th International Conference on Fuzzy Systems and Knowledge Discovery (FSKD), pp. 710–716. IEEE (2015)
7. Bengio, Y.: Neural net language models. Scholarpedia **3**(1), 3881 (2008)
8. Mikolov, T., Chen, K., Corrado, G., et al.: Efficient estimation of word representations in vector space. arXiv preprint arXiv:1301.3781 (2013)
9. Partridge, C., Mitchell, A., Cook, A., et al.: A survey of top-level ontologies-to inform the ontological choices for a foundation data model (2020)

10. Lilleberg, J., Zhu, Y., Zhang, Y.: Support vector machines and word2vec for text classification with semantic features. In: 2015 IEEE 14th International Conference on Cognitive Informatics & Cognitive Computing (ICCI* CC), pp. 136–140. IEEE (2015)
11. Joulin, A., Grave, E., Bojanowski, P., et al.: Fasttext. zip: compressing text classification models. arXiv preprint arXiv:1612.03651 (2016)
12. Zhang, Y., Yuan, H., Wang, J., et al.: YNU-HPCC at EmoInt-2017: using a CNN-LSTM model for sentiment intensity prediction. In: Proceedings of the 8th Workshop on Computational Approaches to Subjectivity, Sentiment and Social Media Analysis, pp. 200–204 (2017)
13. Li, Y., Wang, X., Xu, P.: Chinese text classification model based on deep learning. Future Internet 10(11), 113 (2018)
14. Huang, G., Liu, Z., Van Der Maaten, L., et al.: Densely connected convolutional networks. In: Proceedings of the IEEE Conference on Computer Vision and Pattern Recognition, pp. 4700–4708 (2017)
15. Chen, L., Li, J.: Text feature selection methods based on word vector. J. Chin. Comput. Syst. 39(5), 991–994 (2018)
16. Liu, H., Yin, Q., Wang, W.Y.: Towards explainable NLP: a generative explanation framework for text classification. arXiv preprint arXiv:1811.00196 (2018)
17. Liang, J., Chai, Y., Yuan, H., et al.: Emotional analysis based on polarity transfer and LSTM recursive network. J. Chin. Inf. Sci 29(5), 152–159 (2015)
18. Lu, C., Huang, H., Jian, P., Wang, D., Guo, Y.D.: A P-LSTM neural network for sentiment classification. In: Kim, J., Shim, K., Cao, L., Lee, JG., Lin, X., Moon, YS. (eds.) Advances in Knowledge Discovery and Data Mining. PAKDD 2017. Lecture Notes in Computer Science, vol. 10234. Springer, Cham (2017). https://doi.org/10.1007/978-3-319-57454-7_41
19. Yang, M., Qu, Q., Chen, X., et al.: Feature-enhanced attention network for target-dependent sentiment classification. Neurocomputing 307, 91–97 (2018)
20. Bojanowski, P., Grave, E., Joulin, A., et al.: Enriching word vectors with subword information. Trans. Assoc. Comput. Linguist. 5, 135–146 (2017)

MCPR: A Chinese Product Review Dataset for Multimodal Aspect-Based Sentiment Analysis

Carol Xu[1]($\boxtimes$), Xuan Luo[2], and Dan Wang[3]

[1] Vanke Meisha Academy, Shenzhen, China
xucarol@stu.vma.edu.cn
[2] Harbin Institute of Technology, Shenzhen, China
gracexluo@hotmail.com
[3] Shenzhen Zhenli Technology Co., Ltd., Shenzhen, China
1097400020@qq.com

Abstract. Aspect-based sentiment analysis (ABSA), which aims to analyze the sentiments toward the extracted aspects, has been attracting considerable interest in the last decade. Most of the existing studies concentrate on determining the sentiment polarity of the given aspect according to only textual content, while there is little research on multimodal aspect-based sentiment analysis (MABSA) due to the scarcity of datasets consisting of multimodality content, such as both texts and images. In this paper, we design and construct a **M**ultimodal **C**hinese **P**roduct **R**eview dataset (MCPR) to support the research of MABSA. MCPR is a collection of 1.5k product reviews involving clothing and furniture departments, from the e-commercial platform JD.com. After aspect-base sentiment annotation and text-image matching, we obtain 2,719 text-image pairs and 610 distinct aspects in total. It is the first aspect-based multimodal Chinese product review dataset.

Keywords: Multimodal aspect-based sentiment analysis · Corpus design · Product review

1 Introduction

With the development of e-commerce and express delivery services, more and more people are relying on convenient online shopping. Customers express experiences and share the opinion about service and products in their reviews on e-commerce platforms. The analysis of such reviews plays an essential role in the area of sentiment analysis, enabling some applications like brand monitoring and product upgrading. As an fundamental and important fine-grained sentiment analysis problem, aspect-based sentiment analysis (ABSA) valuable insights to both consumers and businesses [3].

The majority of the existing ABSA methods are dealing with text modal only [3,4], while limited research have been conducted to analyze sentiments

Y. Yang et al. (Eds.): ICCC 2022, LNCS 13734, pp. 83–90, 2022.
https://doi.org/10.1007/978-3-031-23585-6_8

from visual content such as images due to the paucity of multimodal dataset. Nowadays, visual content is becoming popularly used to confirm or emphasize experiences and opinion along with the textual content in the reviews. Such combination of textual and visual content would be beneficial to sentiment analysis toward different aspects. Therefore, Multimodal aspect-based sentiment analysis (MABSA), aiming to perform ABSA based on multiple modalities, such as video, image, text, and audio, has been put on the agenda [7,9,11]. Similar to ABSA, MABSA has several subtasks: aspect term extraction, opinion term extraction, aspect-opinion pair extraction, aspect sentiment classification, etc. [10].

Motivated by the demand of multimodal dataset, a requisite for the advance of MABSA, we design and construct a Multimodal Chinese Product Review dataset (MCPR) for MABSA in e-commerce. MCPR is composed of both text and images from customer reviews. For further study of MABSA, we annotate aspect and sentiment polarity if applicable for each piece of data.

In this paper, we first briefly describe the tasks and datasets within the domain of MABSA in the Related Work. Next, we introduce the design and constuction of MCPR dataset, including its collection, annotation rules and workflow. Then, we analyze the statistics of MCPR dataset.

Finally, we summarize our work in the Conclusion.

2   Related Work

Aspect-based sentiment analysis (ABSA) plays a significant role in sentiment analysis [3]. Depending on the number of the desired output elements, ABSA can be categorized into single ABSA tasks (e.g., aspect term extraction, aspect category detection, aspect sentiment classification, opinion term extraction) and compound ABSA tasks (e.g., aspect-opinion pair extraction, aspect-category-sentiment detection) [10]. Depending on the modality of data, ABSA can be categorized into traditional aspect-based sentiment analysis and multimodal aspect-based sentiment analysis (MABSA).

Most of them focus on performing extraction and classification based on textual content. Recently, MABSA has gained much attention due to the rapid and tremendous growth of many social media platforms, which comprise massive collections of text, images, videos, and audio (e.g., Twitter, Flicker, YouTube, podcasts). Morency et al. developed a videos dataset from popular social media YouTube, which includes 47 videos with transcription [7]. Each utterance was labeled with a sentiment and videos are segmented correspondingly. Zhou et al. built a large-scale dataset MASAD (about 38k samples) for MABSA [11] based on the publicly available Visual Sentiment Ontology dataset [1] and Multilingual Visual Sentiment Ontology dataset [2]. Yu et al. manually annotated the sentiment towards each target of publicly available multimodal Twitter datasets (4k+ pieces in all) for target-oriented multimodal sentiment classification, a subtask of MABSA [9].

For product reviews, McAuley et al. collected a plain text review dataset Amazon Reviews (2013) for recommendation task, including 34.7 million reviews [5]. After that, McAuley et al. incorporated more product metadata, such as images, into the dataset Amazon Product Data (2014), including 142.8 million reviews [6]. Years later, Ni et al. introduced a dataset Amazon Review Data (2018), whose total number of reviews is 233.1 million, adding product images that are taken after the user received the product [8].

However, there is a gap of product reviews and MABSA since most MABSA are studying the dataset from social media while product review dataset are collected for recommendation tasks. Therefore, we build a product review dataset with manual annotation for MABSA to fill this gap.

Img1

Img2

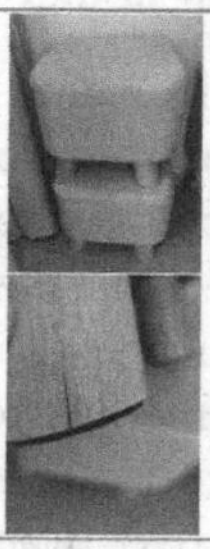

还没坐就开裂了 想着比别人家贵质量待过关吧 两样都不占 啥也不是 It cracked even before I sit on it. I expected a good quality for their higher price. High cost but low performance!	
Reflectiveness	(Img1) 否 | NO
Reflectiveness	(Img2) 是 | YES
Aspect	开裂 | crack
Polarity	负面 | Negative
Expression	还没坐就开裂了 | It cracked even before I sit on it.

Fig. 1. An example from furniture department. The Chinese reviews are translated into English for better presentation.

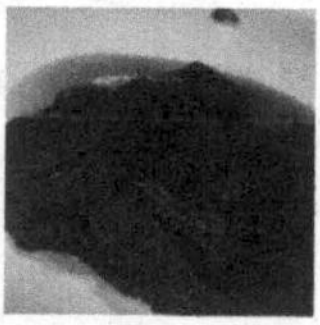

这个裤子，看起来很不错，就是掉色太严重了 This pair of trousers look nice, but the dye bleeds heavily.	
Reflectiveness	是 | YES
Aspect	掉色 | color bleeding
Polarity	负面 | Negative
Expression	掉色太严重了 | the dye bleeds heavily

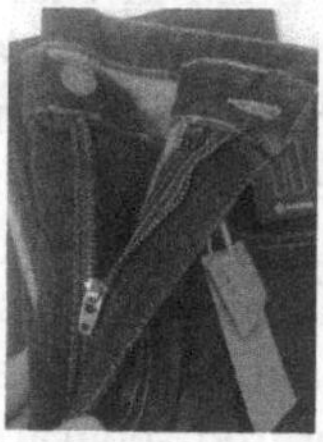

一直穿直筒型牛仔裤，细节处理很到位，ykk拉链很顺滑，基本看不到多余的线头，很满意。 I have been wearing straight-leg jeans; the details are fine; the ykk zipper is very smooth; basically, there is few loose threads; very satisfied.	
Reflectiveness	是 | YES
Aspect	拉链 | zipper
Polarity	正面 | Positive
Expression	ykk拉链很顺滑 | ykk zipper is very smooth
Reflectiveness	是 | YES
Aspect	线头 | loose threads
Polarity	正面 | Positive
Expression	基本看不到多余的线头 | there is few loose threads

Fig. 2. Examples from clothing department.

3   Dataset Design and Construction

3.1   Dataset Collection

We collect our data from e-commerce platform *JD.com*[1]. Among various departments, qualified departments satisfies all of the following criteria:

1) A multitude of reviews with a certain number of negative reviews.
2) The aspect is visible, apparent, and common;
3) Aspects are various;
4) The number of aspect satisfying the above two criteria is more than 5.

Take fruit department as an example. Besides broken or smashed package which is a general aspect, there are several aspects: fresh or stale, rotten, wormy, color, shape, taste, odour, etc. However, taste and odour cannot be displayed in images. Therefore fruit department is unqualified for aspect deficiency.

Finally, we select **clothing** and **furniture** as our source departments. We collect product reviews within these two departments. The media used in product reviews are text, image, and video. We only keep the text and images. The images are related to the item, but are not necessarily reflect the text. Each text-image pair is composed of one image and its review. The number of aspect described in each text-image pair may be zero, one or multiple.

3.2   Dataset Annotation

To better depict the aspect-based sentiment and the connection between images and aspects, we pay attention to the following four attributes:

1) Reflectiveness: whether the images reflects the textual aspect description.
2) Aspect: the aspect described in the review.
3) Polarity: the sentiment polarity toward the specific aspect.
4) Expression: the sentiment expression describing the specific aspect and the sentiment polarity toward it.

We annotate each image with the following workflow:

1) We determine its **reflectiveness** to any aspect described in the text; if it is not reflective to any aspect, skip the rest of attributes. For example, in Fig. 1, there are two images attached to the review. The first image only has reflectiveness attribute annotated since it doesn't reflect any aspect mentioned in the text while the second image has all attributes annotated.
2) We find all the **aspects** related to the image and annotate them one by one. For example, in Fig. 2, these two reviews each contain one image and the second review describes two aspects, which are annotated separately.
3) For each annotated aspect, we determine the **polarity** toward it.
4) For each annotated aspect, we annotate the **expression** that cover the aspect-polarity pair.

---

[1] https://www.jd.com/.

3.3   Dataset Description

Specifically, MCPR comprises 1500+ text-image pairs evenly coming from clothing department and furniture department.

The statistics of raw MCPR is listed in Table 1, and the statistics of annotated MCPR is listed in Table 2.

Table 1. The statistics of raw MCPR. There is only one image in each text-image pair.

#	Clothing	Furniture
Item	38	32
Review	759	759
Total Chinese character	34,358	40,248
Image	975	1,744

Table 2. The statistics of MCPR annotations. There is only one image in each text-image pair.

#	Clothing	Furniture
Reflective : Unreflective	1,196 : 86	2,188 : 148
Phrases w aspect : w/o aspect	1,077 : 119	1,971 : 217
Positive : Negative	613 : 583	1,272 : 916
Chinese character in phrases	9,780	20,754
Distinct Aspects	239	371

For **Clothing** department, we collect 759 reviews with 975 images from 38 items. Each item has 20.0 reviews and 25.6 images on average (759/38 and 975/38). There are 1,196 reflective annotations and 86 unreflective annotations (1,282 annotations in all), namely, 8.8% images are unreflective to their reviews (86/975) and each reflective image displays 1.3 aspects (1,196/(975–86)). Among reflective ones, the number of positive and negative sentiment are similar, with 90.1% aspects mentioned in the text (1,077/1,196). Each review has 45.3 characters and 1.3 images on average (34,358/759 and 975/759), and mentions 1.4 aspects on average (1,077/759). 28.5% characters are describing the aspects and their sentiment (9,780/34,358), with 239 distinct aspects mentioned in text.

For **Furniture** department, we collect 759 reviews with 1,744 images from 32 items. Each item has 23.7 reviews and 54.5 images on average (759/32 and 1,744/32). There are 2,188 reflective annotations and 148 unreflective annotations (2,336 annotations in all), namely, 8.5% images are unreflective to their reviews (148/1,744) and each reflective image displays 1.4 aspects (2,188/(1,744–148)). Among reflective ones, the ratio of positive sentiment to negative sentiment is 1.4, with 90.1% aspects mentioned in the text (1,971/2,188). Each review has 53.0 characters and 2.3 images on average (40,248/759 and 1,744/759), and mentions 2.6 aspects on average (1,971/759). 51.6% characters are describing the aspects and their sentiment (20,754/40,248), with 371 distinct aspects mentioned in text.

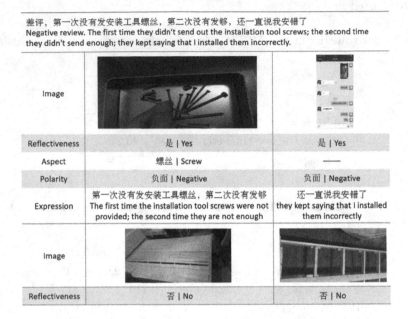

Fig. 3. Another example from furniture department.

Table 3. The statistics of the annotation example.

#	Review in Figure 3
Reflective : Unreflective	2 : 2
Phrases w aspect : w/o aspect	1 : 1
Positive : Negative	0 : 2
Chinese character in phrases	28 (20+8)
Distinct Aspects	1

For instance, in Fig. 3, this review has 4 images and 32 Chinese characters, mentioning one aspect. The unmentioned aspect is annotated as "—". The annotation statistics of this example are listed in Table 3.

3.4 Quality Assurance

MCPR is annotated by three annotators who are familiar with product reviews. Each image and its aspects, polarities, and expressions if applicable are annotated by two annotators working independently. If the two annotations are inconsistent, the image is annotated by the third annotator independently. Then, if two of the annotations agree with each other, we keep the consistent annotations. Otherwise, the whole review containing the image is discarded. Moreover, for simplicity and clarity, we only keep the reviews with apparent sentiment polarity.

4 Conclusion

Multimodal aspect-based sentiment analysis (MABSA) is a challenging task. To support the research in this domain, we design, construct the first multimodal Chinese product Review dataset. We conduct aspect-based sentiment annotation of 1.5k reviews from e-commercial platform. We believe MABSA is a promising and worthwhile domain given its popularity in real-world applications which would help the advancement of brand monitoring, product upgrading, and the e-commerce ecosystem.

Author Contributions. Carol Xu initiates and designs this dataset construction and annotation task, annotates the data and drafts the manuscript. Xuan Luo is responsible for statistics and manuscript writing, and involves in data annotation. Dan Wang makes substantial contributions to data collection and annotation. All authors analyze the annotation ambiguity and approve the final manuscript.

References

1. Jou, B., Chen, T., Pappas, N., Redi, M., Topkara, M., Chang, S.F.: Visual affect around the world: a large-scale multilingual visual sentiment ontology. In: Proceedings of the 23rd ACM International Conference on Multimedia, pp. 159–168. MM '15, Association for Computing Machinery, New York, NY, USA (2015). https://doi.org/10.1145/2733373.2806246
2. Jou, B., Chen, T., Pappas, N., Redi, M., Topkara, M., Chang, S.F.: Visual affect around the world: a large-scale multilingual visual sentiment ontology. In: Proceedings of the 23rd ACM International Conference on Multimedia, pp. 159–168. MM '15, Association for Computing Machinery, New York, NY, USA (2015). https://doi.org/10.1145/2733373.2806246
3. Liu, B.: Sentiment analysis and opinion mining. Synth. Lect. Hum. Lang. Technol. 5(1), 1–167 (2012)
4. Manandhar, S.: SemEval-2014 task 4: aspect based sentiment analysis. In: Proceedings of the 8th International Workshop on Semantic Evaluation (SemEval 2014) (2014)
5. McAuley, J., Leskovec, J.: Hidden factors and hidden topics: understanding rating dimensions with review text. In: Proceedings of the 7th ACM Conference on Recommender Systems, pp. 165–172. RecSys '13, Association for Computing Machinery, New York, NY, USA (2013). https://doi.org/10.1145/2507157.2507163
6. McAuley, J., Targett, C., Shi, Q., van den Hengel, A.: Image-based recommendations on styles and substitutes. In: Proceedings of the 38th International ACM SIGIR Conference on Research and Development in Information Retrieval, pp. 43–52. SIGIR '15, Association for Computing Machinery, New York, NY, USA (2015). https://doi.org/10.1145/2766462.2767755

7. Morency, L.P., Mihalcea, R., Doshi, P.: Towards multimodal sentiment analysis: harvesting opinions from the web. In: Proceedings of the 13th International Conference on Multimodal Interfaces, pp. 169–176. ICMI '11, Association for Computing Machinery, New York, NY, USA (2011). https://doi.org/10.1145/2070481.2070509

8. Ni, J., Li, J., McAuley, J.: Justifying recommendations using distantly-labeled reviews and fine-grained aspects. In: Proceedings of the 2019 Conference on Empirical Methods in Natural Language Processing and the 9th International Joint Conference on Natural Language Processing (EMNLP-IJCNLP), pp. 188–197. Association for Computational Linguistics, Hong Kong, China (2019). https://aclanthology.org/D19-1018

9. Yu, J., Jiang, J.: Adapting BERT for target-oriented multimodal sentiment classification. In: Proceedings of the Twenty-Eighth International Joint Conference on Artificial Intelligence, IJCAI-19, pp. 5408–5414. International Joint Conferences on Artificial Intelligence Organization (2019). https://doi.org/10.24963/ijcai.2019/751

10. Zhang, W., Li, X., Deng, Y., Bing, L., Lam, W.: A survey on aspect-based sentiment analysis: tasks, methods, and challenges. ArXiv abs/2203.01054 (2022)

11. Zhou, J., Zhao, J., Huang, J.X., Hu, Q.V., He, L.: MASAD: a large-scale dataset for multimodal aspect-based sentiment analysis. Neurocomputing **455**, 47–58 (2021). https://www.sciencedirect.com/science/article/pii/S0925231221007931

Author Index

Printed in the United States
by Baker & Taylor Publisher Services